Young Buddies

Teaching peer support skills to children aged 6 to 11

ISBN: 1 4129 1156 7

 Published by Lucky Duck
Paul Chapman Publishing
A SAGE Publications Company
1 Oliver's Yard
55 City Road
London EC1Y 1SP

SAGE Publications, Inc.
2455 Teller Road
Thousand Oaks, California 91320

SAGE Publications India Pvt Ltd
B-42, Panchsheel Enclave
Post Box 4109
New Delhi 110 017

www.luckyduck.co.uk

Commissioning Editors: Barbara Maines
Editorial Team: Mel Maines, Sarah Lynch, Wendy Ogden
Illustrator: Philippa Drakeford
Designer: Helen Weller

© Margaret Collins 2005

Printed in Great Britain by The Cromwell Press Ltd, Trowbridge, Wiltshire.

Young Buddies

Teaching peer support skills to children aged 6 to 11

Margaret Collins

Illustrated by Philippa Drakeford

P·C·P
Paul Chapman
Publishing

Lucky Duck is more than a publishing house and training agency. George Robinson and Barbara Maines founded the company in the 1980s when they worked together as a head and as a psychologist, developing innovative strategies to support challenging students.

They have an international reputation for their work on bullying, self-esteem, emotional literacy and many other subjects of interest to the world of education.

George and Barbara have set up a regular news-spot on the website at http://www.luckyduck.co.uk/newsAndEvents/viewNewsItems

and information about their training programmes can be found at www.insetdays.com

More details about Lucky Duck can be found at http://www.luckyduck.co.uk

Visit the website for all our latest publications in our specialist topics:

- Emotional Literacy
- Bullying
- Circle Time
- Asperger's Syndrome
- Self-esteem
- Positive Behaviour Management
- Anger Management
- Eating Disorders.

Contents

Introduction

Why have a buddy scheme?

'Mentoring, peer modeling and peer monitoring can influence children's behaviour in school corridors and yards, in their homes and in their community environment, bridging the traditional gap between the school and the 'real world'. They reach where the teacher can not be or can not go.'
Topping (1996)

'The practice of befriending, although it can take a variety of forms, is usually focused on enabling the pupils to apply the skills of helping in everyday interactions with peers... what ever the form befriending schemes take, the brief for the young people involved is to offer emotional support and friendship to their peers.'
Cowie and Sharp (1996)

A peer buddy scheme can be beneficial to the whole school. It is thought that peer relationships provide a greater understanding between children, especially where one is older and providing support and one is younger receiving support. These kinds of supportive relationships provide the kind of assistance once found in large families, where older siblings naturally cared for younger ones. In modern families there may be only one child and where there are two they may be too close in age for a supportive relationship to be formed; rather the two siblings may vie for attention from their parents.

Older children often enjoy caring for younger ones; they derive pleasure and increased self-esteem from being in such a supportive role. Younger children are very receptive to older friends and in some cases are more ready to accept the teaching and parenting that such a role provides.

In school there is support from teachers, children in their own class and ancillary workers, yet children seem to get greater pleasure when they experience the different kind of support that only a peer in a different age group can give. To be important to another person, especially from one of the older classes, can give a very different kind of security. Young children feel they really matter to their buddy.

The relationship from the buddy's point of view gives a new dimension to the school day. Within their own class they are one of the herd; they have their own friends and are on an equal footing with them. Give them the responsibility of guiding a younger child in school and they have a whole new role to play – that of teacher, mentor, helper, friend, coach, carer, advisor,

1

guard – the list is endless. This not only increases the buddy's self-esteem, but he gains a sense of worth, value to the school and becomes a useful member of the community. He gains strength as he realises he can not only pass on information about school – the mores and ethos – but also can help the younger child to feel good about herself by accepting the help and encouragement that he, the buddy, offers.

Why use the word 'buddy'?

From the Oxford dictionary:

buddy – '*noun and verb esp. US colloq.* a close friend or mate, *verb* become friendly. [perh. corrupt. of *brother,* or var. of *butty*]'

butty – 1. a mate, a companion, 2. *hist.* a middleman negotiating between a mine-owner and the miners.

Gender and terms

In order to avoid repetition of 'he/she', his/hers, him/her, the word 'he' has been used for the buddy and 'she' for the pal in the main text, although in the scenarios buddies and pals can be either gender.

We also debated the use of the word 'pal' for the young person being helped by the older buddy. If you prefer, you could substitute other words, such as 'chum', 'mate', 'buddymate', 'young buddy' or 'partner'.

The word 'parent' includes other people who care for the child.

New entrants

When new entrants come into school, at whatever age, there is a great culture shock. Reception age children may have had nursery experience, new junior or middle school entrants will have had infant/first school experience, but nothing can prepare them for the vast difference in this new, exciting, frightening, stimulating environment and bewildering collection of so many children.

Nowadays schools make every effort to induct new entrants as easily and sympathetically as possible but there are times when an older and happy child of the school, well used to its ethos, rules and mores, could provide a different kind of support for a sometimes anxious or concerned new entrant.

Young children like to bond with older children – there is a warm security in being told things by another child. In the same way older children enjoy showing the ropes to younger children – it helps the older child to develop in self-confidence and self-esteem and they are close enough to the age of the younger child to know their feelings.

Social aspect

The peer buddying system benefits both the older buddy and younger pal. The pals are able to make easy rapport with their older buddies; they feel secure in accepting help from them and enjoy their interest. It gives the young child someone to call upon, to ask questions of, to feel safe with and to feel important to.

The older buddy has a very important role to play in caring for and empathising with the younger child. They are able to pass on not only the rules and regulations of the school, but also the standards of behaviour, the expectations, traditions and termly activities. Buddies have been successful in school; they are happy and secure – what better role model for a young child who may be nervous or insecure on coming to your school? Being allowed access to the induction of younger pupils will imbue a sense of trust within the buddy as well as in the pal.

Many buddies will easily grow into the responsibility of befriending a younger child and meeting her needs; the increased status will enhance the buddy's self-esteem, quickly developing a friendly yet capable attitude towards their pal. They will all need training in the techniques and qualities needed to do this task well. This book addresses the training of the buddy in an active and interactive way. During this training the buddies will experience practice in life skills; skills that will also help them when they themselves transfer to the next stage of education; skills that will help them in the wider community. Buddies will gain a great deal in self-esteem, stature, status and maturity.

They will also be contributing to the life of the school by:

> ‣ participating in decision making processes
> ‣ taking some responsibility for younger children
> ‣ taking part in peer teaching
> ‣ passing on the ethos and organisation of the school

practising the skills of:

> ‣ acting as a peer supporter or befriender
> ‣ showing they care about other people's feelings

- talking over a problem
- seeing things from another's point of view
- resolving problems or differences by looking at alternatives
- realising the consequences of anti-social and aggressive behaviours
- sharing opinions
- explaining views on issues that affect their school and themselves
- using imagination to understand other people's experiences
- looking ahead at the outcomes of their behaviour

learning:

- about their own and other people's feelings
- that their actions affect themselves and others
- how to respond to aggressive behaviours and when to ask for help
- that there are different kinds of responsibilities, rights and duties at school
- about different kinds of responsibility and how these can sometimes conflict with each other

developing:

- the skills to be effective in relationships
- an awareness of different types of relationships.

Schools that decide not to use the buddy system will find the training programme is broad based and sits well within the citizenship curriculum. Pupils can benefit a great deal from the practice in thinking about others, developing their own self-esteem and awareness of others' feelings. The activities on listening techniques, body language and questioning will serve young people very well as they themselves move on to the next phase of their education.

The activities have been written to help buddies to understand the feelings and needs of their pal and can be easily carried out in Circle Time with the whole class. Circle Time is becoming more appreciated in primary schools as a vehicle for informal discussion. Here, in the round, everyone is equal; the rules allow for each child to have their say while others listen and pay attention. It is not the place here to go into the rules and organisation of Circle Time, but teachers who do not yet fully understand the benefits are directed to the resource list at the end of this book for further information.

Whole-school approach

If your school decides to adopt the buddy system, it must be practised throughout the whole school. After initial staffroom discussions and the acceptance by teachers, you will need to explain the system to governors, non-teaching assistants, parent helpers, mid-day supervisors, cleaners and caretakers. You will need to ensure that parents understand the limited role of the buddy; that it will not take up valuable teaching time from the curriculum but instead give the buddies something extra – another life skills tool.

In most schools the number of children in the buddy class will be almost the same as the number in the pal class and it is proposed that each buddy has one pal. There will be exceptions to this rule and in some cases buddies may have more than one pal, or a pal could have a pair of buddies. The feelings of a pupil in the buddy class who does not want to buddy a pal must be taken into consideration, although if the general expectation is that all children will be included in the scheme, this should not arise. All buddies should do the training.

You may want to hold a parents' meeting to talk about how this scheme will work and to include details of it in your school policy and school development plan. It could also form part of the home/school agreement document and appear in your parent/school brochure. It should be pointed out to parents that the buddy scheme is not to be used for pals from the same family as the buddy.

The training of the buddies should take place during their penultimate term or year at school, so that in their last year they will be qualified to buddy their pal. It will form part of the Physical, Social, Health and Citizenship Education (PSHCE) and can take place during normal lesson times. The training is therefore going to be the responsibility of the teachers of that year group, while the carrying out of the buddying will be the responsibility of the teacher of the following and final year.

School council

If you have a school council you may wish to introduce the scheme to the pupils there. The school council representative of the buddy training year could have a hand in organising and promoting this new venture.

Monitoring and evaluation

Any new scheme such as this will need careful monitoring and the teacher of the final year will want to set aside a special time to allow for this. If buddies visit their pals during the morning break or just before or after on one day of the week, a useful short monitoring time could be immediately after they go back into their own classroom. Teachers may prefer to allocate a special time for this monitoring, perhaps once a month.

A buddy must understand that his pal may well talk about things that are in confidence and must realise that it is not his place to gossip about anything that the pal may say. However, in the unlikely event that a pal discloses a special problem, worry, concern or issue of child protection or abuse, the buddy should know that he must go immediately to tell his own class teacher (unless your school has a different procedure). It is not visualised that the buddy will have direct access to the pal's teacher, but rather conduct any serious concerns through his own class teacher. You will need to decide, and make clear, your own lines of support and communication before the programme starts.

It is expected that any cases of bullying or harassment of pals will be immediately dealt with by the buddy's teacher passing on the concerns of the buddy to the pal's teacher. Should issues of child protection come to light, whether neglect or abuse, the buddy's teacher will immediately act in line with the school's agreed procedures.

A self-evaluation exercise for buddies is included in this book and teachers of the final year may find this useful either as a check sheet for the buddies to complete, or as a check sheet to be used orally during the PSHCE lesson.

Evaluation of the buddy's effectiveness can be made by using the pal's evaluation sheet. This could be done in the pal's class with the teacher going through the paper and discussing each part. If the pal is older and able to read and write well, they could complete the evaluation sheet themselves.

These evaluation sheets, without the children's names on them, could be used by the pal's teacher as a discussion document. They could then be passed on to the buddy's teacher for discussion.

Peer teaching

Peer teaching is a useful tool and you may like to build into your system a session when buddies could read to their pal, listen to their pal read and help with number work – perhaps once a week or once a term. This need not take a whole session and could include the buddy looking at their pal's work and praising and congratulating her on what has been achieved. You could perhaps include pals and buddies in a shared assembly each term enabling a close rapport of the achievement of each group.

Contact time

Buddies also need time with their own friends to engage in their sports and play. It is therefore envisaged that buddies will wear a badge when they are on duty to show when they are available to their pal.

Schools will have to decide for themselves, according to their internal organisation, how contact between buddy and pal can be maintained and how often this should be. Some suggestions follow.

Before the pal comes to school

It could be possible to allow buddies to meet their pals before they actually start school, either at the pre-school visit in the case of new infant children or when the infant/junior class comes to visit the second stage of schooling at their junior/middle school.

In the case of new entrants to infant/first school, parents may be present at this session and the pal's teacher could introduce the buddies and explain their role. They may like to facilitate a meeting between the buddy and the pal's parent.

This meeting could take only a few minutes of the buddy's time and could easily be timetabled to coincide with one of the new entrant's visits at the end of the buddy's penultimate year at school.

When the pal is at school

Initially the pal will need access to her buddy once a week and this can be on a formal or informal basis. As the pal settles into school less contact will be necessary; much depends on the age of the children and their particular needs.

For children who share the same playtime and playground, informal meetings can take place, say, each Monday morning playtime. This meeting could be initiated by the buddy who would seek out his pal and have a chat.

Buddies who do not share playtimes and/or playgrounds could be allowed to visit their pal's playground one morning a week, say for the first or last five minutes of play, depending on their own morning break time.

You may prefer to organise buddies to visit the pal's classroom for ten minutes each Monday morning at some mutually convenient time for an informal chat, to look at work and to read a story.

You may be able to allow the pal to visit the buddy's classroom, say one Friday afternoon each half term, perhaps for all or part of the session after play. During this time the buddy could read a story to the pal, talk to her, play a game, show his own work and talk about his own classroom and organisation.

If the pal has a problem that needs addressing this can be considered at one of these informal meetings. The buddy will decide whether this problem needs addressing by an adult and can approach his own class teacher at the end of the next teaching session.

Other meetings could take place at the instigation of the class teachers, perhaps during special class assemblies, open days or exhibitions of work.

After the first and second buddy/pal sessions it is essential for the class teacher to arrange a reporting back session. This needs to be handled sensitively as the buddy must not feel his vow of confidence to his pal is threatened; rather that the session should look at the practical aspects of the meetings and whether the two are beginning to form a partnership. A simple reporting back format for the first meeting can be found in Section 6.

The training programme

It is suggested that the buddies start their training at the start of the summer term of their penultimate year at school and that the training could form part or all of their PSHCE work for that term. Buddies will meet their pal during this term and start to carry out their duties during the following autumn term; the beginning of their final year at your school.

You may wish to limit the buddying activities to that one term, or allow them to continue for the whole of the year. Whenever you terminate the buddy/pal relationship you could organise a celebration session where buddies, pals and their teachers could meet freely for an integrated session. This could be as elaborate or as simple as you wish. It could be a short 15 minute gathering in the school hall or you could organise an open party session, perhaps even an assembly where buddies and pals could show work and talk about their roles, what they have found useful, how the buddy has helped, how they feel about each other and to which you could invite parents and other friends of the school. Consult buddies and pals; let them organise this celebration themselves. You may like to award certificates of achievement to the buddies and will certainly want to make a note of this on their transfer documents to their next school.

Sample certificates are included in the Appendix on page 106-107.

How to use this training programme

This book is set out in specific sections, with different areas of training. Because of the diverse ways in which primary schools are organised in different counties it has been necessary to split activities so that older infants or first school children can be trained for pals in the reception year. Thus the left hand page has training activities for younger buddies, from Year 1 in Infant schools and Year 2 in First schools, so that they will be qualified to be buddies in Years 2 or 3 (ages 6 to 8). The right hand page has training activities for older buddies, those in Years 5 or 6 (ages 9 to 11) in Primary, Junior or Middle schools who will be qualified to be buddies in Years 6 or 7. This enables a mix and match approach; in some cases teachers of older buddies are asked first to complete the activities for younger buddies. Primary school buddies can use both sets of activities in order to prepare to be buddies for their Reception class. Each section ends with a 'Review and Reflect' page to help the buddies feel successful and good about their training.

It is suggested that teachers allocate a 'buddy board' on a wall in or near their classroom for pieces of information to be gradually added as the training programme progresses. Lists of information, ideas and rules can therefore form the backbone of the work – a kind of 'training manual' for children to refer to. The children are asked to make a buddy folder in which to keep other pieces of work. They will be able to use this work in the final activity when they write their own buddy handbook.

Section 1: The Role of the Buddy

In this section the activities are designed to help children to explore the differences between friends and buddies and to look at locations around the school where they can see their pal.

Buddy folder and buddy board

What is a friend?

What is a buddy?

Younger friends

What is a school buddy?

What does a school buddy do?

How is a school buddy different from a friend?

Where can you buddy?

Buddy folder

Explain to the children that your school is thinking of implementing a buddy system, so that the older children can help the new entrants to settle into school.

Explain that a buddy will be a buddy for a whole term, but that after the term is over, if they still want to be a buddy they can continue until they leave the school.

For the first session, tell the children that you want them to make a folder in which they can keep any interesting and useful pieces of work that they do. Tell them that at the end of this training programme they will have to write a manifesto. This is a piece of paper telling all about themselves and what they can do to be a good buddy to one of the youngest children in school. They will find it useful if they have lots of pieces of work about the activities to help them to do this.

Give each child a piece of paper sufficient to make a folder to hold A4 papers.

Show them how to fold it over and to sellotape or staple the sides together so that it forms a pocket. You can make this activity as elaborate or as simple as you like.

Ask the children to write a name for their folder (My Buddy Folder), to put their name on it and to decorate it as they wish. Remind the children that it is their own responsibility to add pieces of work to this folder.

Buddy board

Explain to the children that you will be designating one of the classroom or corridor display boards as a buddy board and that over this term you will be building up a picture of what a good buddy will do with lots of ideas to help them.

Ask someone to put up some brightly coloured backing paper.

Ask children to make a starter contribution for the board about friendship, helping others and support. These could be in the form of pictures, poems or decorated words about friendship and support and use a variety of media.

Display these on the board – you might like to add a speech bubble, perhaps with an amusing message such as, 'Buddies are training – watch this space.'

What is a friend?

In Circle Time talk about friends and friendship. Ask the children to think about their own friends and what they do together.

Ask volunteers to tell you the things they like to do with their friends. Make a list of these things.

Explain that friends can be family and neighbours as well as school friends and ask the children to finish this sentence about what they do with one friend: 'I have a friend called... and we...'

> ## Friends, we:
>
> play with them
> talk to them
> share things
> help them
> think of them
> read with them
> go to their house
> have sleepovers.

Ask the children to think about what people do to make a good friendship. Remind them about 'give' and 'take' and that friends usually look out for each other.

Ask them to finish the sentence: 'I am good (or kind) to my friend because I...'

Allow children to pass and ask children who repeat what another child has said to change places with the child who last said it. When all have had a turn go back to allow those who passed to have a try.

Collect the things they say and make another list.

Ask them to draw a picture of themselves in a circle and around the circle to draw pictures of their friends. Remind them that friends can be older and younger than themselves and that people in their families can be their friends too.

Share and praise their work before reminding them to put this paper in their buddy folder.

What is a friend?

In Circle Time talk about the role of a friend
and how this role differs according to the
friend and the kind of friendship.

Ask the children to think about how their
friends come from different networks and
how a network of friends works. Ask
volunteers to tell the group about the
different networks that their friends belong
to. Make a list and ask others if they can
add to the list.

> ## Friendship networks
> school
> football
> swimming
> gym club
> dancing class
> netball team
> drama class
> brownies/guides
> scouts/cubs.

Remind them that friends can be of all ages and from different areas of their
life. Ask the children to draw themselves in the centre of a web linking network
and to write on it the names of all the networks to which they belong. Ask them
to add the names of their friends in these networks. It might look something
like this:

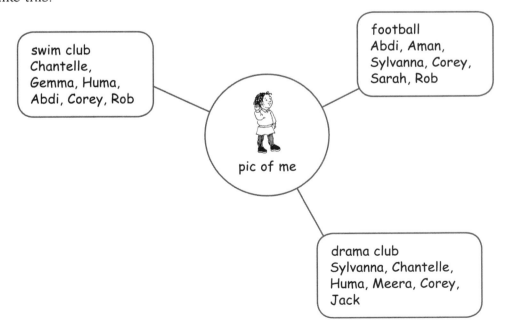

Remind them to put this work in their buddy folder.

What is a buddy?

Ask the children to think what this word
means. Ask them to finish the sentence:
'A buddy is…'

> ## A buddy is:
>
> a friend
> a pal
> your best mate
> someone you like
> someone you want to be with
> someone you care about
> someone you tell things to.

Talk about the things that you do with a buddy,
how you react with them and how you play.

Ask the children whether they think a buddy
has to be the same age as they are – do they
have buddies who are older or younger? Ask volunteers to finish the sentence:
'I have a buddy who is… years old.'

Talk about these people, buddies who are older and younger and ask the
children to think about how they behave with them. Is it the same as the way
they behave with buddies who are their own age?

Ask the children to work in pairs and talk
about the things they do with buddies who are
older or younger than themselves. Ask them
to make a list of the things they do.

A buddy my age

Come back into the circle and discuss what the
children have written on their lists.

Write these headings on a flip-chart or the
chalkboard and ask the children to help you to
make three lists:

1. a buddy my age

2. an older buddy

3. a younger buddy.

Ask the children to draw these buddies and write or tell you the kinds of things
they can do with buddies of these different ages.

What is a buddy?

In Circle Time talk about the word 'buddy'. Ask volunteers to define it. They could use dictionaries. Do they know where the word comes from?

Ask them to give you other words that mean the same. Make a list.

Ask the children to think about where their own friends fit into the categories on the list – do any friends fit into more than one category?

> ### A buddy is:
>
> friend
> mate
> playmate
> workmate
> companion
> partner
> comrade.
>
> 'Buddy' is an American word and means 'a very special, close friend.'

Out of the circle, ask the children to make a list of the categories and write their friends' names in the appropriate place. Remind them that they can include people in their family and neighbours. There may be blank spaces on their lists.

Back in the circle, ask volunteers to tell the group about the people they have included in their lists. Have any included pets?

Ask the children to look at the different ages of the friends they have included in their buddy list. Ask them to draw a ring around the youngest person and the oldest on their own list. Who has the youngest and oldest on their list?

Ask the children to work in pairs and to think about the youngest and oldest buddy on their list and the kinds of things they can do together. Ask one of them to draw their oldest buddy and the other to draw their youngest buddy and to add writing about what they do with their buddies. They can use speech bubbles.

Come together as a group, look at the work and talk about the different ways we all respond to buddies of different ages.

Younger friends

In Circle Time, talk about having friends who are younger than themselves. Ask the children to think about how they talk to and play with someone who is younger than themselves.

What do they do if they can't understand what a very young friend is saying? What kinds of games can they play with a young friend?

Ask the children to think of all the things they can do and games they can play with younger friends.

Go around the circle finishing the sentence: 'I can… with a young friend.'

Talk about how you have to be kind to young friends, especially if you are always winning at a game. Can the children see that they may have to help a younger child to win sometimes?

When with a younger friend:

be fair
play games they can play
help them to win
let them have turns
be kind to them
think of their feelings
don't be bossy
let them choose.

Ask the children to make a list of the things they can do to make things fair when playing with younger children.

Talk about the way that in some games people are given an advantage to make things fairer, for example, sometimes in running sports, younger children start at a halfway point.

Ask the children to give examples of how things can be made fairer for young children who are competing with older ones.

Younger friends

In Circle Time ask the children to think about how they relate to children who are much younger than themselves. Ask them to think whether these kinds of friendships are the same as friendships between children of the same age.

Ask them to finish the sentence: 'Having a younger friend is different because...' and collect what they say.

Allow children to pass and ask children who repeat what someone else says to change places with them. When all have had a turn, ask everyone if they have anything else to add to your list.

Ask the children to think about their role in this kind of young/old friendship, especially where the young child is very much younger than themselves and ask them to think what their responsibilities are. Ask volunteers to tell the group what they think about the roles and responsibility of an old/young friendship.

> **You have to:**
>
> be more thoughtful
> be kinder
> think of their feelings
> make sure they understand
> keep things simple
> use easy words
> give them time
> be patient.

Ask the children to draw themselves playing at home, indoors, with a younger friend. Ask them to draw what they are doing to make sure their play is fair to the younger child and to write in speech bubbles what they are saying.

Come together as a group and ask volunteers to read what they have written about being fair to younger friends when playing.

Can they, as a group, identify the qualities the older friend should display to be fair to a young child so that the friendship will be more even? Make a list of these to add to your buddy board.

What is a school buddy?

I worried about...

mum leaving me
getting lost
new friends
the toilets
school dinners
mum being late
doing things wrong
being told off
the noise
so many children.

Remind the children that your school is going to start a school buddy system and that older children (buddies) are going to help younger children (pals) when they start school. Remind them of the work they did in the previous activities when they were thinking of friends.

Tell them that being a school buddy is not the same as being a friend and it is not the same as playing with a younger child. Ask the children to think back to when they were new at school. Can they remember the things that worried them?

Ask the children to finish the sentence: 'When I was new, I was worried about…'

Make a list of what the children say and at the end ask if anyone can add to the list.

Ask the children to think of one thing they could do to help one of the new children when that pal starts school.

Ask children to finish the sentence: 'I could help a new young child if I…'

Make a list of what the children say and when all have had a turn go through the list with them and talk about how their ideas would work – or how they might not work. Ask them to look at the list and to think which ideas need to be erased and which highlighted. Can they put these ideas in order of importance? Put this list on the buddy board.

Ask them to get paper and pencil and write down which of their suggestions would help young and new children to settle easily at school. Ask them to share this work with the rest of their group before putting it in their buddy folder.

What is a school buddy?

Remind the children that some schools operate a school buddy system where older children such as themselves help new children to integrate into the school system to settle happily and to feel secure at school. Explain that this system can benefit the young children a great deal, but that it also helps older children to be aware of their role in school.

> ## A school buddy is someone who...
>
> helps new children
> tells them about school
> makes them feel good
> listens to their worries
> explains how things work
> shows them around
> is a kind of friend
> bridges the gap between home and school.

Remind the children of previous work when they looked at a buddy and a friend and ask them to think how being a school buddy is different altogether. Ask children to work in pairs and try to identify the role of a school buddy. Can they come up with a definition of what a school buddy is? After allowing a few minutes for discussion ask the children to come together in the circle and ask volunteers to give their definition. Write these down.

Ask the children to look at the list and discuss each part of it. Would all their suggestions work? Do they need to erase some? Can they put the suggestions into order of importance? Have they missed out anything that is important?

Ask the children to work in pairs and draw themselves as a new child at school and to list the things that worried them. Underneath this ask the children to write out the definition of a school buddy. Ask them to write down how a school buddy, as they defined it, could have helped them with some of their own worries. Ask them to write down things that a buddy would not have been able to help them with.

Come together as a group and ask volunteers to read out the last part of their work. Discuss each case and ask whether their definition of a buddy needs to be changed. Display the final definition on the buddy board.

What does a school buddy do?

Ask the children to think about the kinds of things a school buddy could do to help a young pal when starting school. Ask them to finish the sentence: 'A school buddy could…'

Make a list of their suggestions.

When all have had a turn read out all the suggestions and talk about each one to see if it would work. Ask the questions:

'Would this be useful?'

'Would it help the pal to feel good about school?'

'Would it stop them worrying?'

Ask the children to work in small groups or pairs and make three lists of the things that they think they could do:

1. before the pal starts school

2. on the pal's first day at school

3. regularly after the pal has started school.

Come together as a group and share the first list.

Talk about whether these suggestions would work and make a list of those that will.

Talk about their second lists, making one combined list of workable suggestions.

Talk about the third list.

> ## List 1. We could:
>
> meet the pals when they come for a visit
> meet their mum or carer
> say we will be here to help them
> show them around the classroom
> show them the toilets
> show them coatpegs
> tell them about lunches.

Ask each group of children to write up one of the final agreed three lists and display one set of lists under an appropriate heading of the children's choice. Display each list on the buddy board.

What does a school buddy do?

Quickly go through the work suggested for ages 6 to 8 children.

Ask the children to think about all the ways in which they, as a school buddy, could help a pal. Ask them to finish the sentence: 'I could help a pal by…'

Ask a child to be a scribe and make a list on the flip-chart.

Read and discuss the children's suggestions. Cross out any that are not appropriate, practical or possible and highlight those that are essential to a good buddy system.

Now ask them to think about how this kind of buddying will impinge on the ethos of the school. Ask the children to finish this sentence: 'A school buddy system will make the school a better place by…'

Collect and discuss the suggestions.

Ask the children to work in their groups and rule a large piece of paper into two columns. Head one column, 'It will help me' and the other, 'It will help the pal'. Ask the children to write their ideas with a thick pen so that others can easily see what they have written.

Allow enough time for the children to write several ideas before sharing what they have written with the other groups. A good way to do this is to display the large sheets of paper on a wall or table and allow other groups to visit. One member of the group should stay behind to explain what is meant by the writing.

It will help me	It will help the pal
I will have to relate to younger children.	They will feel happier being helped.
I will think about their needs.	They won't feel so alone.
I will be aware of their feelings.	They will know someone cares.
I will know how they feel.	They can talk over their troubles.
I will feel good about doing this.	They won't be so scared of us big ones.

How is a school buddy different from a friend?

Remind the children about the work they did about friends and buddies. Ask them to think about how a friend, a buddy and a school buddy are different.

Ask them to finish this sentence: 'A friend is…but a school buddy is…'

Collect their responses and make two lists.

Ask them to think about choosing friends – what do they look for in a friend?

Ask the children to work in pairs, talk about how they choose them and write down a list of what they look for in a friend.

Ask them not to put their names on their papers, shuffle them and read to the whole group. Ask the children to decide on the suggestions that are valid, to delete any that are not and to agree a final list.

Talk with the children about school buddies and pals and the different kind of friendship in this situation.

Ask the children to work in small groups and write down the qualities of a school buddy/ pal relationship. Ask the groups to choose a spokesperson to read out their list to the class.

Again delete any suggestions that are not valid and agree a final list. Display the two lists on your buddy board.

School buddies

You don't choose them.
You don't meet out of school.
You help them settle in.
You don't get a close friendship with pals.
You help them to help themselves.
It's not an equal partnership.
You teach them about school.
You support them.
You listen to them.
You don't tell them your troubles.
You tell them how to get other help.

How is a school buddy different from a friend?

Go through the work for ages 6 to 8 then extend it with these activities.

Explain that there may well be some situations where they themselves will not be able to help their pal and will have to do something else. Explore these ways in Circle Time through the following scenarios by asking volunteers to suggest solutions. List their suggested solutions and discuss after each pair of scenarios.

Friend	Pal
Your friend is having trouble with his work. He keeps on getting things wrong and playing about and the teacher gets annoyed with him. What could you do to help your friend?	Your pal is having trouble with his work. He says he keeps on getting things wrong and the teacher says he is playing about and gets annoyed with him. What could you do to help your pal?
Your friend is having problems with someone being unkind to her in the playground and says it is bullying. What can you do to help your friend?	Your pal says she is having problems with someone being unkind to her in the playground and says it is bullying. What can you do to help your pal?
Your friend is worried about his homework and is always in trouble at school for not doing it. What can you do to help your friend?	Your pal tells you she can't do her reading and no-one will help her at home. What can you do to help your pal?

Have you helped your children to see that there is a lot they can do to help a friend but that there is a limit to the kind of help they can give their pal? Help them to understand that their role in being a buddy is to help the pal to talk about the problem and decide for herself what to do. Sometimes the buddy will be able to suggest someone else who the pal can ask to help them.

Where can you buddy?

Ask the children to think of discrete ways they
can show they have seen their pal as they
move around the school.

Make a quick list of these ways to put on the
buddy board.

Ask them to think of your school playground
and dinner hall as two good places where they
can informally see their pals and to think what they can do in these two areas.

See your pal? You can:
nod wave a hand smile do thumbs up raise your eyebrows mouth 'hello'.

Ask the children to work in pairs or small groups and jot down suggestions of
how they can do their buddying in these two places in your school.

Playground	Dinner hall
Once a week, on Monday mornings, buddies and pals can get together to have a short talk or play.	Pals and buddies might be able to meet occasionally in the dinner hall. This depends on the arrangements for the meal.
They need to explain to their pals that they are entitled to play with their own friends and cannot spend too much time with their pal.	Sometimes older children supervise younger children at the meal and this might enable buddies and pals to meet.
Depending on the layout of playgrounds they may be able to keep an eye out for their pal during some playtimes, but pals have to make their own friends too.	When they are on the same table some contact such as a smile or wink may be sufficient.

Come together as a class and ask them to share their ideas to make fuller lists.
(Make sure that they understand that they are only part time buddies and that
they must have time to be with their own friends.) Ask them to display the lists
in a grid similar to the one above.

Make sure it is applicable to your school and display it on your buddy board.

Where can you buddy?

Work through the activities for ages 6 to 8 and then expand this by asking the children to list all the other places where they might be able to do their buddying.

For example, the library, music room, medical room, art room, after school group activities, after school sports teams.

> ## Where else?
>
> on the way to school
> after school when the
> children disperse
> in school shared assemblies
> in shared reading times
> during wet playtimes
> during wet dinner times
> in the school library
> in the art/music room.

Explain that when their pal first comes to school they will feel very vulnerable and that a smile or a nod from their buddy will be very reassuring. Remind them to make sure that they are aware of their pal as they move around the school, and that when they pass by they should initiate eye contact with a smile or nod.

Ask them to work in pairs and choose two other areas of the school where they might meet their pal. Jot down how they can behave towards their pal in these areas of your school. Come together as a group and make a list of all their suggestions. Delete those not really appropriate and make a final grid similar to the one below to go on your buddy board.

Classroom	Lunchtime playground
We can't do our buddying in the pal's classroom because the teacher is in charge there.	In our school, buddies can sometimes spend a very short part of the lunchtime play together.
When we (buddies and pals) get together for meetings in the pal's classroom we buddies might be able to help to solve small problems.	Buddies are on a different meal sitting from pals but share the same playground. Buddies can play on the football field but not younger children who might get hurt. On wet dinner times some of us can visit our pal's classroom and play with them there.
In cases of real problems buddies must tell our own teacher who will be able to help by talking to the pal's teacher.	

Review and reflect

Spend a little time with the children reflecting on the work they have done. Ask them to think about what they didn't know before they started this programme.

Ask the children to turn a piece of A4 paper to landscape and make three columns. Head the columns thus:

1. What I thought being a buddy was.

2. What I now know about being a buddy.

3. What I think I still have to learn about being a buddy.

Ask them to write down their thoughts under these headings.

Read through the work on your buddy board and ask the children if they can add to these.

Ask the children to design an illustrated certificate of intent, saying why they would like to be a buddy and how they would try to carry out their duties.

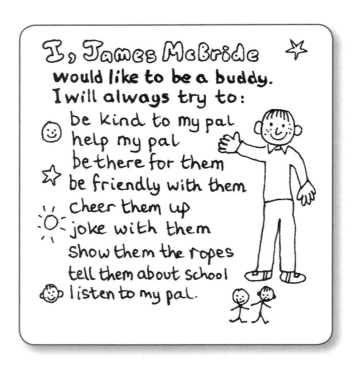

Section 2: Aims, Skills and Techniques

In this section the activities are designed to help children to explore the various skills and techniques they need to enable them to be an effective school buddy.

The aims of the buddy scheme

What skills does a buddy need?

Listening skills

Not listening

Body language

Questioning techniques

Empathy

The aims of the buddy scheme

Talk to the children about setting up the buddy scheme and ask them to think of why this would be a good thing for your school. Tell them that a scheme such as this has to have definite aims and that their task today is to think of the aims of the buddy scheme.

Ask the children to finish this sentence: 'I think the aim of a buddy scheme is to…'

Allow children to pass and ask those who repeat to change places with the person who said it first.

Make a list of what they say and then ask everyone if they can add to the list.

Ask the children to work in pairs and to put this agreed list into order of importance to keep in their buddy folder.

We will aim to:

help pals to settle
show them around
let them know we can help
listen to their worries
tell them about school
explain the rules
be there for them
show them how we behave at this school
make them feel good.

Choose one of the lists to display on your buddy board.

Now ask the children to think of how helping pals can help them, themselves, to become better people. Can they see that doing this good work will help them to learn to get on with people and be a useful member of the school?

Ask them to think of how being a buddy could change them.

Ask them to work in pairs and write their own list of how it will make them feel to be a buddy. After five minutes or so, ask them to get together with the rest of their group and share these ideas, putting them on one piece of paper. Ask them to choose a spokesperson who will read their list to the class.

Come together as a class to share the lists. Help the group to select from these lists the components for an agreed class list. Ask them to think of a title for this class list and ask someone to write it out neatly to put on your buddy board. Ask the children to put a list of the aims into their buddy folder.

The aims of the buddy scheme

Explain to the group that when setting up any new scheme it is important first to identify the aims. Talk about aims for other organisations, such as a swimming club or a football team.

Ask volunteers to identify the aims of one of these outside school organisations.

Explain that aims usually begin with the word 'to' and ask them to work in pairs to identify the aims of a buddy scheme in their school. Ask them to make a list

Ask them to share their list with others in their working group and to choose the best aims to make one list. Ask them to write out this list on a large piece of paper and to display this on a wall or table so that other groups can visit, read and talk about their lists.

In a whole group session identify the most important of these aims and ask someone to use the computer to create a list. Talk about how these aims will help the young pals to feel good about being in their school.

Now ask the children to think about how being a school buddy will help them to develop their own skills. Repeat the above exercise, this time concentrating on the aims of the scheme and how it will help them to develop as sensible and caring members of your school. When you have their final aims, add these to the computer generated first list to display on your buddy board. Ensure the children put a copy of each list in their folder.

> ## Buddy system aims:
>
> to help new children when they first come to school
> to help them to understand the rules
> to help them to feel part of our school
> to help them to know how we behave
> to help them with any worries
> to be there to listen to them
> to be a safe person for them to consult.

> ## More aims:
>
> to help us to develop as caring members of school
> to improve the ethos of the school
> to develop our own self-confidence
> to play a part in the development of the school
> to take responsibility for the needs of others by acting as a peer supporter
> to be a good role-model.

31

What skills does a buddy need?

Talk to the children about the need to be a good buddy to their pal.

Remind them that being a buddy is different from being a friend and that they will need to practise being a buddy so that they will be able to do this well.

Ask the children to think of what they will need to do and to be. Ask them to finish the sentence: 'I think a buddy needs to…'

When they repeat what someone else says ask children to change places with the person who said it last. Make a list of what the children say. Can they add any more?

> I'm listening
>
> ## Buddy skills
>
> listen to them
> talk to them
> get them to talk
> be friendly
> nod to them
> smile at them
> show you're interested
> talk about work
> explain the rules
> help them to feel good.

Ask the children to work in pairs, with one being the buddy and the other being the pal. Ask the children to pretend that the pal is unhappy about coming to school and the buddy has to try to find out what is the matter. Allow the children five minutes or so to do this role-play and then ask them to come together to talk about this (without changing roles).

Ask volunteers to say what was easy and difficult about this role-play.

Ask volunteers to tell the group how they managed to get their pal to talk.

Talk about ways of getting children to open up and talk about their problems.

Ask the children to work in the same pairs, but to change over and role-play the pal who says she hasn't any friends.

After five minutes or so, come together as a whole group and talk about these role-plays. Ask children to vote whether they thought they managed to help their pal or whether they felt they didn't know what to say. Explain that later in this programme they will be helped to develop skills to help them with situations such as this.

What skills does a buddy need?

Ask the children to think about the personal skills they will need to develop if they are to become a useful buddy for their pal. Ask volunteers to finish the sentence: 'I think a buddy has to be a person who…'

Ask a member of the class to be a scribe and write down these skills on the chalkboard or flipchart. When everyone has had a chance to contribute, read out the list and talk about the most important skills and the least important. Ask the class to suggest a numbering system with the most important skill as number 1. Re-write the list to display on your buddy board. Ask each child to put a copy in their folder.

Prepare a set of cards – similar to playing cards. Ask children to write a different skill on each card. Shuffle the cards and read out the top one. Ask two volunteers to role-play the situation while others watch. Discuss.

Remind the children that some of the skills they will be developing will help them to become more effective in relationships and to:

> The skills of:
>
> communication
> showing you care about other people's feelings
> seeing things from other points of view
> recognising different responsibilities
> understanding rights and duties at school
> talking over a problem
> acting as a peer supporter or befriender
> showing you understand other people's experiences
> suggesting alternative solutions
> looking ahead at outcomes of behaviour
> explaining that actions affect themselves and others.

▸ use imagination to understand other people's experiences

▸ participate in the school's decision-making process

▸ prepare themselves for the move to their next school

▸ become better citizens, all round, in the community.

Listening skills

Remind the children that one of the skills they
said they would need to develop in order to
be a successful buddy is to be an effective
listener. Explain that it is not sufficient to
hear the words; they must make sure they
understand what their pal is meaning by the
words they use.

Remind them that their pals are not yet really
good at explaining things – they do not know
enough words and sometimes use the wrong
words to try to say what they mean. Remind
them also that they will have to show their
pals that they are really listening and that this
is not easy to do. Ask the children to think
about how they show they are listening to
someone. Ask volunteers to finish the sentence: 'To show you are listening
you can…'

> Hmm.
> I see.

I'm listening…

sit facing them
look at their face
concentrate
nod & say 'Yes', 'Mmm'
say 'I understand
don't interrupt
show interest
ask questions
encourage them to continue
by repeating their last
words.

Ask someone to write out this list on the computer to display on your buddy
board. Leave a space so that more things can be added.

Ask the children to work in pairs, with one as the pal and the other as the
buddy. Ask the pal to pretend they have a problem such as not wanting to eat
their school dinner in the dinner hall because of the noise. Ask them to explain
their problem and ask the 'buddy' to show that they are really listening.

Allow a few minutes and then come together as a class. Ask volunteers to say
whether this worked or what they need to practise so that it will work. Remind
the buddy to make sure the pal knows they are really listening and to practise
the things from the list. Change over roles and use the same problem.

Remind the children that this skill of showing they are listening can be used in
all kinds of places and situations.

Listening skills

Remind the children that in order to be an effective buddy they will need to sharpen up their listening skills. Explain that they will not only have to listen carefully to hear their pal's message, but that they may have to decipher it if their pal is not yet a good speaker.

Ask the class to think about why we listen. Ask volunteers to make suggestions and ask someone to scribe a list of why we listen. Read through the list and discuss it. Do the children need to re-word it? Display the final list on your buddy board and ask children to put a copy in their folder. Talk about how important it is to hear what the pal means when they use the words they do.

Why we listen

to help them
to hear what they say
to understand what they mean
so they will tell us things
to understand their problem
so we can suggest alternatives
so we can help them with a problem
because it's important to them
because they need us to.

Ask the class how they can make sure they understand what the pal means. Are there strategies they can use to make sure they really understand what their pal is trying to say to them? Ask them to work in their groups and write down on separate pieces of paper all the things they can do to show they are listening and to show they are paying attention to the meaning of what the pal is saying. Collect these papers to read their list to the whole class. Ask them to help you to discard repetitions and put the rest in order of importance.

There is a list of effective listening skills at the end of the book. Make sure that most of these are on your class's list and then display it on the buddy board with a copy for their folder. Ask volunteers to tell you what would make their pal think they were not listening, for example, looking away or fiddling with things; no eye contact.   Ask the children to work in pairs and to role-play a scenario where the pal is anxious about getting to school late. Change over roles and discuss. Ask the class to remember the good things that aid communication and the things that hinder it.

Not listening

Remind the children about the listening activities in the previous activity. Tell them that today they are going to practise listening, showing that they are listening and showing that they are not listening.

Ask the children to think of a time when they knew that someone was not listening to something they wanted to tell them. Ask volunteers to tell the class what happened and how they felt.

Make a list of these feelings and ask children to add to them. Now ask the children to think about how their pal might feel if they weren't really listening to her when she talked to them about her life in school. Would the pal have the same feelings as they did when someone didn't listen to them?

When people don't listen we feel...

sad
angry
unwanted
a nuisance
no good
useless
that they don't care.

How do people know that you are not listening? Ask volunteers to tell you the signs of people not listening, such as looking away, watching other people, not looking at them, no eye contact, drumming their fingers, leaning back, calling out to other people.

Ask the children to work in pairs, one to be the pal telling the other (the buddy) about the problem of feeling unhappy in the classroom while the buddy displays some of these 'not listening' techniques. Change over roles.

Come together as a class and talk about how the pal was feeling when their buddy was not listening. Ask a volunteer to write out a list of these feelings on the computer. Choose a good heading and display the list on your buddy board with a copy for each child's folder.

Not listening

Remind the children of the previous activity about listening skills. Ask them to think of a time when they had something really important to say and the person was either not there, too busy or just not listening. How did this make them feel? List these feelings.

Tell them that you are going to give them practice in not listening. Ask the children to work in pairs, one the teller and the other not listening. Ask them to talk for two minutes about the thing they like best about school. Remind the listener to make sure they show that they aren't listening. Change over and this time ask them to talk about the best party that they ever went to.

> ## I would feel...
> frustrated
> angry
> fed-up
> irritated
> upset
> annoyed
> cross
> bad-tempered
> as if I were useless
> let down
> thwarted
> unimportant.

Come together as a class and talk about how the talker felt when he knew he wasn't being listened to. Ask volunteers to give you words to express this. Now say you want to collect the 'feelings words' of the talker when he wasn't being listened to. Add these to the first list.

Now ask the children to think of what the listener was doing so that the talker knew he weren't listening, for example, no eye contact, no nods, no encouraging words, smiling at someone else. Ask volunteers to say what these were and ask someone to make a computer list of these distractions to display on your buddy board and give copies to each child for their folder.

Ask the children to think about external distractions – the things that could be going on to stop the listener paying attention, for example, an aeroplane roaring overhead, too much noise or other children milling about. Remind the children to bear all this in mind when they are listening to their pal.

Body language

In Circle Time, remind the children of the listening skills they have been learning when talking with their pal. Explain that as well as showing they are listening by their face they can do this by their body language. Ask the children to think what body language is. Ask volunteers to tell the class, by finishing the sentence: 'I think body language is...'

> **Body language**
>
> how you use your body
> how you sit
> how you move
> your position
> your movements
> careful touches.

Make a list of what the children say.

Tell the children you are going to practise some body language. Ask each child in turn to 'pass their body language' around the circle and to show by their body (including their face) how they feel when they are:

- ▶ feeling good   ▶ upset
- ▶ feeling sad   ▶ surprised
- ▶ angry   ▶ excited.

Make sure everyone has the chance to observe everyone's body language. Talk about using body language as a way to communicate.

Ask them to find a place in the classroom where they will not touch anybody or anything and all together to show the same feelings as they stand.

Ask them to find a partner, choose which will be A and which B so they can work together making a 'conversation' along these lines...

A is very unhappy; B shows they care about this. Change over.
A is very excited. B shows they understand this. Change over.
A is worried about something. B shows empathy, touching A's hand.

Ask the children for other suggestions to end the session.

Explain to the children that showing this kind of body language helps people to feel comfortable about communicating their feelings.

Body language

Ask the children to try to list the ways they can use body language to show they understand the feelings of their pal. Ask the children to finish the sentence: 'To show you feel for them, you could…'

> ## Using body language
>
> watch their movements
> watch their posture
> look at their hands
> look at their face
> mirror their movements
> mirror their posture
> show by your face and
> posture movements that you
> understand
> gentle touching
> sympathetic smiles, nods
> leaning forward
> use gestures.

Allow children to pass and use the change places technique for repeats.

Make a list of these ways of using body language. Read through the list and then practise each of these body language movements as you sit.

Ask children to work in pairs, A and B.

> A looks dejected in face and body. B mirrors it. Change over.
> B shows sympathy in face and body. A mirrors it. Change over.
> Talk about this – does mirroring help?
> A adopts an angry 'things aren't fair' body language. B soothes.
> B adopts an excited lively face and body language, A empathises.

Come together to talk about how the children felt when doing this. Did it help them to show their feelings to the other? Did it help them to empathise?

Ask the children to work through this scenario with a different partner.

> The pal has a problem with going out to play. She feels that the playground is a hostile place and doesn't know where to go in order to be safe. She would like to stay inside but they are not allowed in. She wants help.

Ask the children to play one of the roles and without speaking to try to convey the worry that the pal is experiencing. The buddy can mirror the body language of the pal and try to convey sympathy while helping the pal to cope with this problem. Explain that it is not easy to do this at first, but that they can practise with friends at home or in the playground until they become experts in this kind of body language communication.

Questioning techniques

In Circle Time tell the children that you are going to try to help them to know how to use different kinds of questions when trying to help their pal. Tell them that there are open and closed questions and ask volunteers to try to tell the group the difference.

Yes

Questions

Open questions have lots of answers and closed ones only have 'yes' or 'no'.

Ask the children to think of a closed question – one that has only the answer 'yes' or 'no'. Start off with you asking a closed question to the person nearest to you. Ask them to ask a closed question to the person next to them and so on until everyone has had a turn. Repeat the exercise, this time with an open question.

Talk about the different kinds of answers you get from these questions and ask the children to think which will be of most use for a buddy to use to a pal.

Ask the children in pairs to role-play this scenario with one as the buddy and one as the pal. Ask them to use only closed questions and to make a note of these.

> The pal is angry because someone is not being fair in their classroom. This person keeps on spoiling people's work and making a noise when people are working. The pal has come for advice because she wants to know what to do when other children keep spoiling things.

Come together as a class and talk about the kinds of open questions that would be useful in this scenario. Ask the children to change over and use only open questions. Ask them to tell you what they were.

> Do you feel better now you've told me?

> How did that make you feel?

> What did you want to do?

> What did other children say?

Discuss the benefits of using open rather than closed questions.

Questioning techniques

Quickly go through the open and closed questioning techniques for the younger age group and make sure your children understand the difference by doing the activity.

> ## Questions
>
> You can use...
> 'why?' questions
> leading questions
> multiple choice questions.

Ask the children if they can think of other kinds of questions. Ask volunteers to give their suggestions and make a note of these.

'Why?' questions are easy – they all start with 'Why' and intend the answer 'because…'

Leading questions usually imply the answer you are seeking and don't give the other person much of a chance to think of their own answer, for example, 'You're not going to do that are you?'

Multi-choice questions have several alternatives for the person to choose, such as, 'Would you rather go home, go to the medical room or go back to your own classroom?'

Discuss the different uses of these kinds of questions and ask the children which they think are most useful.

Practise using them in the classroom. In Circle Time give each child a number: one, two or three. Tell all the 'ones' they have to ask a why question, all the 'twos' ask a leading question and the 'threes' ask a multi-choice question. If you have time you can re-number the children so that they get more practice.

Explain that different occasions need different kinds of questions and ask them to think of examples of when each kind of question would be best. Ask the children to work in pairs and to write down three scenarios when each question would be the best way to help a pal.

Add your list of types of questions to your buddy board as a reminder to the children. Ask them to make a note of different kinds of questions for their folder.

Empathy

I feel for you

Tell the children that when they are trying to help their pal
the most important quality they can display is
that of empathy. Ask volunteers to say what
they think this word means. Discuss with
all the class what empathy means. Ask the
children to work in their groups to write down
their own definition in their own words.

Empathy means...

showing you put yourself in
their place so you can feel
what they feel.

Ask each group to choose a spokesperson to
read out their definition to the class. Collect in their papers and at the end
read them all out again. Ask the children if they can use the best ideas from all
these to come to agreement of one definition. Ask someone to write this up to
display on the buddy board.

Use the following scenarios to help the children to work in pairs, buddy and
pal, to practise the skill of showing empathy.

Your pal is not feeling well; he was sick this morning and didn't want to come to school. His mum goes to work so the teacher can't send him home. ▸ What can you do? ▸ What can you say?	Your Pal's dad is going away to work and he says he will be missing her. She looks really sad. ▸ What can you do? ▸ What can you say?
Your pal is feeling very upset because her cat is lost and they can't find it anywhere. ▸ What can you do? ▸ What can you say?	It's your pal's birthday and she is having a party. She is really excited. ▸ What can you do? ▸ What can you say?

Remind the children that when they are in their buddy role they should always
be thinking of the pal's needs, never their own.

Empathy

Tell the children that one of the skills of being a good buddy is being able to show empathy towards their pal. Ask them to tell you what this word means. Give them four minutes to work in pairs to do this. They can use a dictionary. Ask volunteers to read their definitions and use their contributions to agree on one that you can display on your buddy board.

Empathy means...

the power of identifying oneself mentally with (and so fully comprehending) a person or object of contemplation.

Explain that it is not always easy to put yourself in someone else's shoes, but that practice will help. Ask the children to work through these scenarios in pairs. Tell them that at the end you will want volunteers to talk about their feelings about these scenarios.

Jacob was saving all his money to buy his mum a present for her birthday. He was going to the shop to buy it and must have pulled out the note with his tissue and has lost his £5.	Shallon has had toothache for a day or so and her mother has made her an appointment to go to the dentist. She has to go this afternoon after school and she feels quite ill at the thought.
▸ What could you say to Jacob?	▸ What could you say to Shallon?
▸ What could you do?	▸ What could you do?
▸ Can you suggest any ways to help him?	▸ Can you suggest any ways to help her?

Remind the children that when they are in their buddy role, they should be thinking of the pal's needs, never their own.

Review and reflect

Spend a little time reflecting on the work the children have done. Ask them to think about what they didn't know before they started this section of activities.

Ask the children to make two columns on a piece of A4 paper. Head the columns thus:

1. aims of being a buddy
2. new skills and techniques I have learned.

Ask them to make a brief list under each heading.

Now ask each child to make a drawing of him or herself being a buddy using one of these skills or techniques. Ask them to write what they are doing and how it could help their pal.

Section 3: Responsibilities

In this section the activities are designed to help the buddy to look at some of the responsibilities of being a buddy and how he can carry these out. We help buddies to identify signs of things not being well with the pal, such as worries, bullying and pals with special needs.

Feelings

Responsibilities

Getting to know you

Observing

Worries

Bullying

Special needs of pal

Feelings

Remind the children of the need to keep calm and in control of their feelings when they are with their pal. It is important never to over-react. Tel the children that today you are going to talk about feelings and ask them to close their eyes and think of as many good feelings as they can. Ask them to finish the sentence: 'A good feeling is…'

Allow children to pass, but give opportunities at the end for additions. Ask 'repeats' to change places. Call these positive feelings and make a list of them.

Negative feelings

anger
dislike
hatred
ill-feeling
sadness
hurt
being upset
frustration
irritation
fury
rage
annoyance
fed-up.

Now ask the children to think about bad feelings – about how they feel when things are going wrong or when they are not happy about things. Call these negative feelings.

Ask the children to think of what could happen if they went to meet their pal feeling one of these good feelings. Ask them if they think things would be different if they were feeling one of these negative feelings.

Ask them to get a piece of paper and fold it in half. On one half ask them to draw a picture of themselves going to meet their pal with one of the positive feelings and to write about what could happen at the meeting. On the second half ask them to draw a picture of themselves going to meet their pal with one of the negative feelings and to write what might happen then. Come together as a class and ask volunteers to show their pictures and to read out what they have written. Can the children see how important it is for them to be in a positive frame of mind when meeting their pal?

Talk about how the meeting might go if the pal was feeling any of these negative feelings. Ask volunteers to finish the sentence: 'If my pal had negative feelings, I could…' Talk about each volunteer's contribution and whether it would work.

Remind the children that when they meet their pal, they must be in charge of their own feelings and think only about their pal's needs.

Feelings

Talk with the children about positive and negative feelings. Go through the activities on the previous page. Using the two lists of words they have suggested, make (or ask the children to make) two sets of feelings cards in different colours – one set with positive feelings and one set with negative feelings. You are going to need sufficient of each kind for each pair of children, so make some duplicates to make sure that there are enough.

Ask the children to work in pairs and each pair pick one card from the positive feelings pile and one card from the negative feelings pile. Ask them to find a quiet place in the classroom and work out a role-play, with one person acting the buddy, the other the pal with the buddy having the positive feeling and the pal the negative feeling. Come together as a class and ask volunteers to show their role-play. Discuss what happens in the role-play when the buddy is positive. Talk about how buddies can help pals to become calmer and happier.

> When I was the buddy with negative feelings, my pal became sad and upset.
>
> When I was the buddy with positive feelings my pal became happier and we had fun.

Ask the children to return to their quiet place and act out the role-play with the opposite feelings, with the same person being the buddy and the same person the pal. This time the buddy uses the negative feelings card and the pal has the positive one. Come together and discuss the role-play. Ask the children what kinds of meetings these negative feelings have generated.

Ask each pair of children to use both sides of the A4 paper; on one side to write down the heading 'buddy positive' and on the other 'buddy negative'. Ask them to write about how the buddy performed in these roles. You may like to play around with these feelings cards and role-play with both feeling positive and both feeling negative.

Remind the children that the buddy is in charge of all meetings and that whatever feelings he has will be communicated to the pal.

Responsibilities

Ask the children to think what the words
'responsible' and 'responsibility' mean. Ask
volunteers to say what they think. If they
find this difficult, ask them if they can use the
word in a sentence, for example, 'A teacher
is responsible for the children's learning',
'Children are responsible for taking care of
their reading books when they take them
home', 'A buddy will be responsible to try to
help their pal to settle into school and feel
good about coming'.

Responsibilities   see you!

to be friendly
to meet her often
to listen
to be fun
to help
to explain things
to show her around
to keep confidences.

Ask them if they can tell you some of the other responsibilities they will have
as a buddy. Ask them to finish the sentence: 'As a buddy I will be responsible
for…'

Make a list of these things and when everyone has had a say, read through the
list, adding any others that the children may have not thought about.

Ask the children to write these responsibilities on small cards and if necessary
duplicate some so that there will be one card for each pair of children.

Ask the children to think of how they can carry out their responsibilities and
ask volunteers to suggest a few ideas. Ask each child to choose a partner,
shuffle the cards and give one card to each pair.   Ask them to role-play the
situation on the card with one being the buddy and the other a pal.

Go around the groups and encourage them for about ten minutes or so. Come
back to a circle and ask volunteers to show their role-play. Emphasise the
importance of what they say, listening, questioning and positive body language
as they carry out this role-play. Ask them to change roles, choose another card
and do the activity again.

Responsibilities

Talk about the responsibilities your class have as older children in the school. Ask volunteers to list theirs.

Talk about the responsibilities your class have within their families. Ask volunteers to list theirs. Be aware of any children in your class who are in either foster or residential care.

Now talk about their responsibilities as a buddy. Ask the children to work in their groups and make a list of all the responsibilities they think they will have towards their pal. Ask them to cut up some paper so that they are about playing card size and to write one responsibility on each card.

Come together into a circle and collect all their cards. Read through the cards, putting to one side any duplications.

> ## Buddy responsibilities:
>
> make relationship work
> give advice about school
> listen to worries
> encourage her to think
> act as role-model
> explain how he can help
> bridge the gap between home/school
> as peer tutor
> give support to her needs
> motivate her thinking
> show her around
> pass on the ethos of school
> explain the rules
> show that we carry out the rules
> respect her.

Ask the children if they can help you to put the cards into order of importance and lay these out on the floor in the centre of the circle. Encourage a discussion of their order and accept several in first or second or last place.

Ask someone to make a list of these, in this order, for the buddy board.

Collect and shuffle the cards and deal them out, one to each pair of children. Ask them to go and write a dialogue between a buddy and a pal that will show they are carrying out the responsibility well.

Back in the circle ask volunteers to talk through their dialogues; encourage discussion from all as to how well they carried out their buddying responsibilities.

Getting to know you

In Circle Time, tell the children that they will have to learn the skills of getting to know people they haven't met before. Tell them that when they meet someone they don't know and want to get to know there are certain things they can do and say.

Explain that they are going to this today and that you will start them off. Tell the children a little about yourself – things such as your favourite books, plays, TV programmes, what flowers/plants you like and one of the things you like to do when you are not being their teacher.

> My partner told me that she likes to help in the garden at home, but she hates weeding.

Now ask the children to work in pairs and to think of all the things they can tell their pal about themselves that will help them to get to know each other. Ask them to write these down so that they will not forget. Back in the circle collect and share all the children's ideas.

Make a combined list of all the topics to display on your buddy board.

Ask the children to look through the list and pick out two good things to say to people when you want to get to know them. Ask them this time to work with someone they don't know very well, someone in a different group. Ask them to take it in turns to tell their new partner the two things from the list. Remind them to listen to each other, to pay attention and to keep good eye contact.

> My partner told me that he likes to go to the skating rink in town. He goes every Saturday.

Back in the circle ask each pair to stand up in turn and say one of the things that their partner told them.

Ask them to find a different partner and practise this skill by choosing another two ideas from the list.

Ask them to make a copy of the good ideas to put in their buddy folder.

50

Getting to know you

Go through the activities on the previous page and build upon these by asking the children to make a list of all the things they would like to say to their pal when they first meet her.

> I'm going to be your buddy and I will come to see you every week. We can talk about lots of things, but first I want to tell you a bit about me. I have two sisters and a dog. Have you any brothers and sisters?

Ask volunteers to stand up and say what they would say to their pal about buddying. Explain that it helps if they tell something about themselves and then ask a question about that to the buddy.

> your name, your siblings, your birthday, your hobbies, your favourite TV programme, about pets, holidays, books, favourite lesson, music, what you are good/not so good at, things you like to eat and drink, going to picnics, BBQs.

Tell the children that you want them to work in pairs and to use this 'tell and ask' technique, but first ask them to help you to make a list of all the kinds of things that they could tell their pal about themselves.

Come together and ask the children to think about their buddying role and how to find out about the needs of their pal. Ask them to start with, 'Tell me...' and make a list. Have they included things such as:

▶ how you like school   ▶ about the work you like

▶ if you have any problems   ▶ about the work you don't like

▶ if you find it hard in your class   ▶ about your new friends at school

▶ what you enjoy most   ▶ about yourself in the playground.

Ask them to work with a partner and practise these opening sentences. Can they think of any more to add to the list? For example, 'Tell me about yourself'.

Display the list on the buddy board. Ask them to think of a good heading for the list, such as, 'Getting to know you'.

Observing

In Circle Time talk to the children about the need for good observation when working with their pal. Do the children know what the word observing means?

Ask volunteers to raise a hand and tell you what they think it means. Jot down what they say on the flip-chart and then read out the list. Are all their suggestions correct? You may need to add your own. Display the final list on the buddy board.

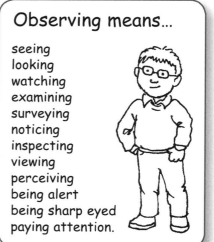

Observing means...

seeing
looking
watching
examining
surveying
noticing
inspecting
viewing
perceiving
being alert
being sharp eyed
paying attention.

Ask the children why they think that buddies need to observe their pals. Ask volunteers to put a hand up and after each suggestion, discuss with the whole group whether the child is correct.

Explain to the children that it will be their job as a buddy to observe if their pal is not settling well at school or is unhappy or worried about any aspect of school, inside and outside.

Talk about the various things that they can try to observe:

▸ general appearance – school uniform, generally clean and tidy

▸ facial expression – happy and secure

▸ body language – positive and happy

▸ how they act with, and react to, their peers

▸ how they talk about school and work

▸ whether they appear to have friends.

Tell them that they can help their pal by talking to them about what they have observed and that in a very careful way they can question their pal if they see something that does not seem right. Remind them that if buddies observe or find out something worrying about their pal and they can't help they must tell their class teacher who will help.

Observing

In Circle Time you may like to go through the activities for the younger children. Talk to the children about their role as observer of their pal and explain that they have a very particular part to play in noticing anything that may seem to be not well with their pal.

Ask them to think about the things that they might notice that could cause them to think that all may not be well with their pal. Ask them to finish the sentence: 'I might notice that my pal…' (add 'looks', 'feels', 'seems', if the children are not able to continue).

> ## My pal might...
> look unhappy
> look tearful
> look dirty
> have torn clothes
> look hungry
> seem worried
> seem friendless
> be always late
> have no lunch
> have no coat
> have no PE kit.

Talk with your class about what they can do if they notice that things don't seem right with their pal. Ask them to think of all the sensible things they can do and to work in pairs to make a list.

Ask them to show their list to the rest of their group and make a new list of all the sensible things. Come together as a class to discuss all the items on the lists. Are they all sensible options? Would some be difficult to do or might people be angry if buddies tried to put things right in this way?

Make one agreed list of all the sensible things to do and ask one child to type it out on the computer and print it out for the buddy board.

Ask them to work in pairs and role-play these scenarios:

> Jonno has come to school for several days without his PE kit.
> Mim keeps forgetting to take her reading book home.
> Sam looks unhappy and is always playing on his own.
> Raja jumps when people rush by him.
> Sara looks anxious when she knows it's time to go in to dinner.

Come together and discuss the correct thing for a buddy to do in your school if these things happen.

Ask the children to write a message of what to do when something is too worrying for them to cope with and to display this on the buddy board.

Worries

In Circle Time remind the children that they have thought about listening skills, body language and empathy and ask them about the kinds of things that they think might cause their pal to be worried or anxious at school.

Ask them to finish the sentence: 'A pal might be worried about...'

Allow children to pass and to change places for repeats.

Jot down these worries and when everyone has had their turn read through the list with the class.

Now go through the list again, asking volunteers to say what they can do to help to make their pal feel less worried in each case. Use different colours to identify worries that:

‣ they can make the pal feel better about by being light-hearted and joking

‣ they need to question the pal about to find out more information

‣ they need to chat about with friends of the pal

‣ are too difficult for them to help with and need adult help.

Ask the children to work in pairs to write down what they would do in the following cases. Ask them not to put names on papers.

Your pal is crying because she has forgotten her lunch box.
Your pal is upset because the teacher has been cross with her.
Your pal is fighting because she says her friends are all horrid.
Your pal is sulking because she has lost her reading book.

Collect the papers and read out the children's suggested solution for the first problem. Jot down these suggestions and ask volunteers to comment on them. Ask the class to vote on which solution they think is the best. Work through the other three scenarios in the same way.

Remind the children that their role is to help their pal when they can, but that there will be times when they need to ask an adult for help.

Worries

In Circle Time, go quickly through the teaching points on the previous page. Build on these by talking about the kinds of things they can do to help their pal.

First, find out what is wrong
Remind the children what they can say to try to find out what is wrong, such as, 'Tell me what is wrong', 'I can see you're upset, what's the matter?', 'Come on, you can tell me!'

Second, making sure they know what the problem really is
Ask the children to clarify what the problem is by repeating what the child has said and waiting until the pal confirms, remarks such as, 'I think your problem is…', 'So what's really wrong is…'

Third, making suggestions
'Could you do this…?', 'Have you thought about doing this…?', 'What about doing this…?', 'You could always try this…?', 'What could happen if you do this…?'

Fourth, help the pal to work out how to do it
'Could you be doing something wrong?', 'How do you think the others feel?', 'What is the best thing to do first?', 'So, how will you go about it?', 'Do you think you need a grown-up to help you?'

Fifth, do you need to enlist adult help?
Who are you going to go to for help? Is your pal happy about this?

Ask the children to work in pairs and use these five steps to sort out the problem of a pal coming to school late every day saying that her Mum never gets up in time. She is always in trouble with the teacher because of this.

Ask the children to think of other scenarios where a pal is unhappy and to use these steps to find the best way to help. Remind the children that after trying to help to solve a problem it is up to them to find out if their pal is feeling better about it or whether they still need to seek adult help for them.

Bullying

Remind the children about the last session when they learned to observe the behaviour and actions of their pal. Talk about bullying and how they might notice if this was happening to their pal.

Bullying is...

hurting people for no reason
doing it again and again
calling names
teasing or taunting
saying horrid things
taking or breaking things
keeping children out of groups.

Remind them that young children often say that someone is bullying them when it is, in fact, not bullying at all, but rough play that is uncomfortable for them.

Ask your class to think about what bullying is and what bullying isn't. Ask them to work in pairs and to make a list of bullying actions. Ask them to share their list with the rest of their working group and to put their lists together to make one longer list.

Come together as a whole class and ask a spokesperson from each group to read out their bullying list. Talk about whether these really are bullying or not and if some are not bullying actions make a second list of not bullying actions.

Talk about what the buddy can do if they think someone is being unkind or hurtful to his pal, for example, explain that it is not bullying, feel empathy, ask his pal what would be a good thing to do, suggest several things the pal can do or say and ask her to decide which is best for her. Ask the children to choose the best things to do and say and write each on a small card. Shuffle the cards and ask two volunteers to role-play these situations while others watch. Practise with other cards and other children.

Make sure that the children know what a buddy must do if he thinks his pal is really being bullied. He must tell his class teacher.

Bullying

Talk about some of the work from the previous page and about the difference between hurtful behaviour and bullying.

Discuss the bullying policy in your school and what you have to do if you see someone bullying someone. Make sure everyone knows that they must tell their class teacher if they think or know someone is bullying their pal. Make sure that the children know the difference between bullying and not bullying and that they only take this step if they feel sure that their pal is really being bullied.

Ask the children to think of all the different kinds of bullying they can. Ask them to work in their groups, decide whether these scenarios are bullying or not and come to agreement about what they should do.

> Your pal is upset and says she is being bullied. When you ask her about it she says that those two boys won't let her play with them; they just shout at her and say, 'Go away, you, you can't play with us, it's a boy's game!'
>
> Your pal is looking unhappy and when you ask her what is the matter she says that a girl in her class is always pushing her and sometimes it makes her fall over. You ask her if this has happened only once or more than once and she says that the girl is always doing it.
>
> Your pal says that the boys in the class are always calling her names because she has a scar on her face. When you ask her why she thinks they do this, she says it's because they are horrid. You ask her how many boys are involved and she says that it's all of them.

Come together as a class and talk about what your children think about these three scenarios and what they would do. Have they come to the correct decision? Make sure the children realise that they have a responsibility to act even if these scenarios are not bullying. Ask them to work in pairs to devise other scenarios and say how they would act.

Make sure they understand and pass on the message that this kind of behaviour is not to be tolerated in your school.

Special needs of pal

In Circle Time, explain to the children that though we are all the same in very many ways, each of us is unique and special. Ask the children to think about this and to finish the sentence: 'We are all the same because…'

Now ask them to think of the ways in which we all differ from each other and ask them to finish the sentence: 'I am different and special because I have/am…'

Now ask the children to think about children who are very different from the children in your class, children who have health problems or who have special difficulties. Ask volunteers to tell you some of the ways

> ## Children who
>
> have an illness
> use a wheelchair
> use inhalers
> have difficulty with work
> can not see properly
> can not hear well
> can't write well
> go to hospital a lot
> can't speak clearly.

that children can have special needs. Make a list of these, talking about the uniqueness and special difference of each child and the way each may have to be treated more carefully and in a special way.

Remind the children that there may be some pals who have special needs and that these children will need particular help from their buddy.

Ask the children to work in pairs and to write down the kind of special needs that three pals might have. Ask them to list the ways in which they could help pals such as these.

Come together as a class and talk about these ways of helping special pals. Remind them that it is their job to make sure that all pals feel good about themselves and about coming to school and that if their pal has special needs, it is even more important that they remember this.

Special needs of pal

Tell or remind your children about the work for younger buddies on the previous page. Explain that they may never have a pal with special needs but that they need to be aware of how to help such people to feel good about themselves.

Ask the children to work in pairs with one role-playing a pal in a wheelchair and the other role-playing the buddy. Ask them to think carefully about what the buddy will say to the pal. Change over. Ask them to write down the kinds of questions or remarks they might say to the pal in the wheelchair that will show that they understand how the pal feels.

Come together as a group and look at the questions or remarks that the children have written down. Ask the group to think about whether some of these might make the pal feel sad or whether there are some that would make the pal feel great. Will any help to raise the self-esteem of a pal with special needs? Make a class list of all the positive things a buddy could say to make a wheelchair-bound pal feel good about herself.

> ## What would YOU say
>
> Would you like me to push you or would you rather move yourself?
>
> Shall we see if we can join in the game of those children over there?
>
> You are really doing well using your new chair – how does it feel?
>
> You're ever so good at getting about on your own. Don't you feel great?
>
> Could we join in that ball game if I push you?
>
> Would it help if I carried that or shall we put it in your lap?

Ask the children to help you to make a list of other illnesses or conditions that make some children very special.

Ask the children to repeat the wheelchair exercise with a pal who has one of these conditions or illnesses.

Come together and talk about the importance of building up the self-confidence and self-esteem of all pals, especially those with special needs.

Review and reflect

Spend a little time reflecting on the work the children have done. Ask them to think about what they didn't know before they started this section of activities. Remind the children that they have been looking at some of the responsibilities of being a buddy and how to carry these out.

They have been thinking about observing, worries, bullying and pals who may have very special needs.

Ask the children to draw lines half way across and half way down a piece of A4 to make four boxes. Ask them to write one of these headings in each box.

- ▸ One thing I have learned about observing.

- ▸ One thing I have learned about worries.

- ▸ One thing I have learned about bullying.

- ▸ One thing I have learned about people with special needs.

Ask them to choose one of the above and to draw themselves on the back of the paper doing the most important thing they think they have learned through the activities in this section.

The most important thing I have learned is about children with special needs. You have to think how they would feel before you say or do anything that could make them feel bad.

Section 4: Buddying, Not Friendship

In this section the activities are designed to help children to understand the difference between the casual role of friendship with their peers and the more professional role of a buddy. It is important for the pal to feel secure with her buddy and that everything will be confidential unless there are child protection issues or the pal agrees to involve other people.

Boundaries

Distancing

Keep a distance

Confidentiality

Disclosing

Boundaries

Explain to the children that there are boundaries to their role as buddy and that they must make sure that they do not overstep the boundary lines.

In Circle Time, ask the children to recap on the role and responsibilities of a buddy. Now ask them to think of the kinds of things they cannot do for their pal and ask volunteers to raise a hand to tell you. Jot down their suggestions on a flip chart. Read through the list and discuss each one. Cross out any that you think the buddy can do and add any more ideas of things that a buddy mustn't do.

Ask the children to work in pairs to role-play one of these scenarios with one being the buddy and the other the pal:

A buddy isn't:

a parent
a teacher
a nurse.

A buddy cannot:

take on a pal's worries
always sort out problems
tell a pal what to do
make the pal do things
always be there
do her homework
help her at home
visit the pal at home.

Scenario 1

The pal tells her buddy that she is really angry because the teacher has made her sit at a different table where she has no friends. The pal is really upset and the buddy can hardly understand what the pal is saying.

Scenario 2

The pal is laughing and joking about someone in their class who was in trouble this morning because they had done something wrong. She tries to tell the buddy all about it, but she is laughing so much that the buddy can't really hear.

Come together as a class and ask volunteers to tell you what happened in the role-play in both these cases. What would be the best things for the buddy to say and do in each case? In Scenario 2, what can the buddy say to help the pal to be more understanding and kind?

Boundaries

Talk the children through the activities on the opposite page, highlighting the responsibilities of the buddy in setting the boundaries.

Ask the children to work in their groups to discuss these situations. What is the best thing for the buddy to do in each case? Come to an agreement about what you think is the best thing to do. If you can't come to an agreement, write down the alternatives.

You get on well with your pal and want to buy her a present at the end of the term because you are leaving. Do you think you would be stepping outside the boundaries – would it make other buddies think they ought to give a present? What is the best thing to do?
Your pal says that she is always being sent to bed without her supper because she cannot do her homework. Her dad gets really cross and sometimes smacks her. She says she hates her dad and nobody loves her. She cries and asks you to help her. What should you do?
Your pal is going to have a birthday party at the swimming pool next Saturday. She asks you to go. You'd like to go, but you aren't sure about the boundaries. Who can you ask about the right thing to do?
Your pal always wants to kiss and cuddle you. You're not sure what to do about this as you don't want to reject her, but it doesn't seem quite right in a buddy/pal relationship. What can you say to stop this so as not to hurt her feelings?
You have seen your pal behaving very badly towards a little boy in another class. She pushes him about and taunts him. You're not quite sure if you should do anything. When you talk to your pal about this little boy she just says he is a wimp. What should you do?

Come together as a class and talk through what the various groups have said is the best thing to do. Can you agree as a class the one best thing to do in each case? Write a careful list of the things to do in situations like these so that it can be displayed on your buddy board. Make a record that can be kept in the buddies' folders.

Distancing

Remind the children about the work they did about the differences between friends and buddies. Explain that the role of the buddy is a professional role and not really one of friendship.

Ask the children to think of the difference between being a friend and being friendly. Ask them to work in pairs, to fold a paper in half, to write the headings and a definition of 'Being a friend' and 'Being friendly'.

> Being a friend means you work and play together and think about them a lot. You tell them your secrets, you share lots of things with them.
>
> Being friendly means you are happy to talk to people. You are usually cheerful and interested.

Ask them to share these lists with the rest of their group and to make one list that they all agree on.

Back in the whole group, ask a spokesperson from each group to read their list and ask the group to comment on these contributions.

Remind the children that being friendly is the role they should play with their pal; they should be open, helpful and good to their pal, but they have to step aside and not think of their pal as a friend.

Ask the children to work in small groups and to make a list of all the things they do with their friends. Come together and share these lists, making one complete list. Now ask the children to work in the same small groups and make a list of all the things they do to be friendly. Come together and share these lists, making one complete list. Draw a ring around the words/phrases that are on both lists.

Explain to the children that their role as a buddy is quite different from their role as a friend. It's a one way friendship; they need to keep a little distance between themselves and their pal. Help them to understand the difference.

Distancing

You may like to go through the activities on the previous page to set the scene for this part of the training programme.

Ask the children to think of their role at home, with their parents or carers. Are they friendly to these people? Take a show of hands.

Ask if they are a 'friend' to these people. Take a show of hands.

Ask the children to think of their role as a pupil at school with you, their teacher. Ask the children if they can see that while they are friendly with you, their teacher, they are not a friend.

> ### A buddy is like a:
>
> teacher
> helper
> coach
> confidant
> mentor
> advisor
> listener
> questioner
> advisor.
>
> A buddy is not the same as a friend.

Ask the children to work in pairs and to make a list of people they are friendly with – not using people's names, but their jobs or positions. Ask them to share this list with their working group and try to put all their lists together to make one list. Come together as a class and ask a spokesperson from each group to read them out. Can all the class see the difference between being a friend and being friendly?

Talk about the buddy/pal relationship. Explain that this is a very special kind of friendship, but that their role is different from being a friend. They must try to keep a distance between themselves and their pal.

Ask children to volunteer to finish this sentence: 'A buddy is a… to their pal.'

Make a list of what they say and talk about whether you all agree. Come to a consensus and write up a class list to display on your buddy board.

Keep a distance

Remind the children about the activities they did about distance and say this is one of the main differences between a friend relationship and a buddy/pal relationship.

Tell them that when their pal tells them about their likes, dislikes, problems, joys that they may be tempted to tell the buddy things about themselves. Explain that this is OK as long as they don't treat the pal as a friend and tell them things that are unnecessary, using the relationship for their own purpose instead of a way to help their pal and make them feel good.

Ask the children to work in pairs and to talk through the following scenarios and decide which would be good practice and which not.

Your pal tells you about her worries at getting hurt in PE lessons. You say that you once got hurt and say what happened when you fell off the ropes and how much your leg was bleeding, so you went to the medical room and had to have treatment. You tell them about the First-Aider who had to bandage up your knee and how much it hurt.	Your pal tells you about her worries at getting hurt in PE lessons. You say that it hardly ever happens, but that if it did, someone would make sure you were helped to feel better. It once happened to you and the First-Aider made it OK in no time. 
Your pal tells you that she feels afraid and lonely in the playground. You say that you will help her to find a friend to play with and ask her about the children who sit on her table for work. She points out two of the girls and you take her over and suggest a game they can play.	Your pal tells you that she feels afraid and lonely in the playground. You say you used to feel like that and sympathise with her. You say it gets better as you get to know more children and that it will be OK then.

Ask your children to suggest other scenarios like these and to point out the good and not so good things to do.

Keep a distance

You might like to use the previous work as an introduction to this idea that they need to keep a professional distance between buddy and pal.

Talk about the usefulness of using some of their own experiences as a bridge to sort out a pal's worries. Explain that this can be a useful bonding technique, but only if they stop short of clouding the issue or using their pal as a sounding board for their own self-importance. Ask the children to work in their groups first to discuss this and then write down two examples of good practice and say where it could go wrong.

> ## You could say...
>
> Yes, I felt like that once.
> Oh, I know how you feel.
> We all feel like that sometimes.
> That happened to me.
> Don't...
> scare them by going into your problem
> forget to listen to them
> go on about how it hurt you
> bore them with your problems.

Ask the children to work on their own to write down a good and not so good response to these scenarios. Ask them not to put their names on their papers and say you will want to talk about their anonymous responses in Circle Time.

Your pal has eczema on her hands and some people won't play with her. A good response would be...	Your pal has eczema on her hands and some people won't play with her. A not so good response would be...
You pal is afraid to go to the toilet because the door doesn't close and she doesn't like people to see her. A good response would be...	You pal is afraid to go to the toilet because the door doesn't close and she doesn't like people to see her. A not so good response would be...

Ask the children to work in pairs to discuss other problems that a pal might have and to suggest good and not so good responses. Share these in Circle Time.

Confidentiality

Talk to the children about their relationship
with their pal. Tell them that they must not
talk to other people about what their pal says.
Explain that their role is to be like a counsellor
to listen and try to help, but not to gossip
about what their pal says.

Ask the children to think about how they
would feel if they told their special friend
a secret and their friend went and told
everybody. Ask them to finish the sentence:
'I would feel…'

Collect their words to make a list of all these
feelings.

I would feel…

upset
sad
angry
ashamed
people might laugh
betrayed
they were disloyal
I couldn't trust them
they had let me down
I wouldn't want to tell them
things again
my friend isn't really a good
friend.

Talk about gossip – that sometimes it can be true gossip and could be harmless
fun, especially if the people concerned didn't mind other people knowing.
Explain that sometimes it can be untrue gossip which could hurt people or
make them angry.

Ask the children to think of things their pal might say which they would want to
keep confidential, for example, worries about their teacher, things about their
home or their families. Ask the children to work in their groups to discuss and
make a list of the kinds of things that pals might say that were confidential and
must not be passed on or gossiped about. Share these in Circle Time.

Now think of the things that they ought to pass on to other people. Explain
that they would have to tell their pal that they were going to tell someone in
school about this so that they could help them. Explain that buddies should
always ask their pal's permission before telling someone they could trust, but
in a serious case they would need to pass on the information even if the pal
didn't agree.

Confidentiality

Use the activity on the opposite page as a starter and explain that you want them to examine their professional role as a buddy. Talk about the kinds of things that you could share with other buddies – your pal's successes, their happiness, the way being their pal makes you feel.

Ask volunteers to tell the class of other things that it would be good to share with their own friends.

Talk about the things that are, or should be, confidential about being a buddy. Make a list of things you wouldn't gossip about. Read through the list and pick out any that could be talked about in a kind way, for example, if a pal had a new jacket that she was proud of, if the pal was really funny about some new shoes or if the pal told a good and kind story about a sibling.

> ## You wouldn't gossip about...
>
> their clothes or their accent
> their race or religion
> their family circumstances
> their failures
> them being very rich
> them being very poor
> where they live
> their parents or carers
> their special needs
> their illnesses
> any disfigurement
> them being dirty.

Ask the children to work in their groups and make a grid, writing four of the things from the list in the left hand side and a space on the right for them to write good things they could do or say. The first two might look something like this.

Her failures	If a pal talks about her failures you could cheer her up by saying you would help her. You could say that it's often hard when you start something new and ask her to think about what she can do to be better at the thing. Say, 'Don't worry, I won't tell anyone.'
Her parents or carers	If a pal talks about her parents or carers, you could ask her to tell you what she likes best about these people and what they do to show they care about her. Say, 'I don't talk to other people about what you tell me.'

Read out and discuss the suggestions with a whole class. Can they all agree on the best things to say and do?

Disclosing

Remind the children about the last session when you were talking about confidentiality. Ask the children to think about whether there is ever a time when they should tell someone about what their pal has told them.

> ## You have to tell if your pal is...
>
> being bullied
> taking things
> doing something against the law
> hurting people
> hurting herself
> afraid of someone
> bullying someone.

Ask volunteers to finish the sentence: 'You would have to tell someone if...'

Collect what the children say to make a list.

Read through the list with the children and ask if they would always have to tell someone if they knew this was happening. Are there some things that they can cross off the list? Are there more things they could add?

Tell the children that if any of these things were happening to their pal, they have a responsibility to tell someone. Ask them to think about what they would say to their pals about this.

Ask children to work in their group and write down the actual words they would have to say to their pals. Share this with the whole class and make one list of what they could say. Ask children to try to number them in order of importance.

Ask the class to think about who they should tell and where and when they should do this. Ask them to work again in their groups and try to come to agreement about the best people to tell, where to do this and when. Ask a spokesperson to tell the class.

Discuss what each group thinks and try to come to agreement as a class about this. Ask someone to write this down (or use the computer) to go on your buddy board. Ask the children to make a note of this in their folders.

Disclosing

Ask the children to find out what the words 'disclose', 'disclosure', 'disclosing' and 'disclosed' mean. Allow them to use dictionaries and give just a few minutes for them to do this. Bring the class together to listen to the suggestions.

> If your pal discloses something worrying, you, in your turn, must disclose to someone you trust.

Remind the children of the last session about confidentiality and ask if there is ever a time when they must disclose what a pal has told them. Ask volunteers to give their suggestions. Write these up. The list will be similar to the one on the previous page, but these older children may add more serious situations.

Explain to the children that their role with their pals is to support and to listen. Only the child protection officer is allowed to ask questions to clarify. The pal's teacher is in charge of their pal for most of the day. However if their pal discloses anything that is worrying or of concern, it is the buddy's duty to report this to someone. Tell them that they must be fair to their pal and explain to them that they have to do this.

Ask the children to work in pairs and make a list of all the people in school they can trust if they have to tell something worrying about their pal. Share the lists to make one list. Cross off anyone that you should not tell and put the rest in order of importance. It will probably end up with just two names – you, the buddy's teacher and the headteacher (if you are absent), unless you have agreed that the buddy can have access to the pal's teacher.

> ## Should you tell these people?
>
> my friend
> the school council rep
> my teacher
> the headteacher
> the school secretary
> the school nurse
> my pal's teacher
> my parents
> the pal's parents
> the classroom assistant.

Remind the buddies that (unless your internal arrangements differ) they must tell you immediately if they think that something serious is wrong with their pal.

Review and reflect

Spend a little time reflecting on the work the children have done. Ask them to think about what they didn't know before they started this section of activities.

The activities have been helping the children to understand the difference between the casual role of friendship with their peers and the more professional role of a buddy. They have been thinking about the issues of confidentiality, boundaries and disclosures.

Ask the children to think of the one most important thing they have learnt in each of the activities and to complete these sentences in writing:

▸ The most important thing I learnt about boundaries is...

▸ The most important thing I learnt about distancing is...

▸ The most important thing I learnt about confidentiality is...

▸ The most important thing I learnt about disclosing is...

Ask the children to celebrate the end of this section by drawing a picture of themselves as a buddy doing something that shows they really understand the difference between buddying and friendship.

This is me making sure I don't overstep the boundary when I am talking with a pal. I'm sitting close, but not crowding her.

Section 5: Positive Action

In this section the activities are designed to help the buddy be positive in the relationship with his pal and to be a good role model.

Peer teaching

Helping your pal to make decisions

Feelings of both buddy and pal

Role models

Peer teaching

Ask the children to think about ways they could help their pal with their work. Remind the children that the pal's teacher is in charge of their learning, but that pals will need to practise the skills they are learning. Ask the children to finish the sentence: 'I could help my pal with…'

Remind the children about the boundaries of buddying and that they may well not be welcome in their pal's classroom and taking up the class teacher's time.

Ask the children to think about the actual help they can give and to work in pairs to write down how they could actively give help in the following situations:

> ## I can help by…
>
> listening to reading
> reading to them
> helping with number work
> testing spellings
> talking about homework
> being interested
> talking through problems
> helping them to remember
> looking at their work
> seeing displays in their class
> encouraging them.

> You see your pal every Monday morning at break time and she is always anxious about her spelling test that day. It is too late to help her with this week's spellings because the test is always first thing after break. What could you do to help her next week?
>
> Your pal says her paintings are not very good and never get put on the classroom display boards. She usually takes them home but her mum just looks at them and throws them away. Is there any way you could help?
>
> You know that your pal keeps forgetting to take her reading book home and practise there. Is there any way you could help her to remember?

Come together as a class and ask for their solutions. Would these all work? Are they appropriate and practical?

Ask the children to work in their groups and to write down two more situations where they think they could help in peer teaching with their pal. Talk about these situations and decide whether these ideas are practical in your school.

Peer teaching

First work through the ideas on the opposite page. Talk about the informal kind of peer teaching in those activities and ask them to think whether some kind of peer teaching could be arranged in a lesson time.

Ask the children to think about the organisation of your school day, their timetable and identify spaces where it would be possible to peer teach their pal. Ask volunteers to finish the sentence: 'We could peer teach in...'

Come together and discuss whether any of these ideas would work. Now ask the children to work in pairs and to write down the constraints:

▸ Would the pals like this and would they benefit?

▸ Would the pals' teachers like this and would they benefit?

▸ Would your own teacher like this and could the teacher see some benefit?

▸ Would your own work suffer as a result of time spent this way?

▸ How much time each week would this need?

Come together as a class and discuss each separate question.

Ask the children to go back into their pairs and work out how they could make peer teaching possible, bearing in mind the school timetable, the weekly organisation and the different sections of each day. Ask them to come up with an acceptable and practical plan for your school.

After five minutes, ask them to share their plans with the group and to put their ideas together to make a new plan. Ask them to write this plan out on a large piece of paper to display on a wall or table. Ask the children to visit each group in turn, to read their plans and to come up with one foolproof plan that they think would benefit everyone in the two classes – teachers and children. Display any acceptable plan on the buddy board.

Our peer teaching plan

We could use half an hour after play each Friday afternoon and go to our pal's classroom to set up peer teaching groups. We could all listen to our pal read, look at her books and displays and pick out good work to praise. Both our teachers could be there and we could spill out into the corridors or library if it was cramped.

Helping your pal to make decisions

Explain to the children that one of their roles is in helping their pal to think through problems or situations and help them to work out for themselves an acceptable solution. Remind them that their role is never to tell their buddy the best thing to do, only to act as a listener and to help them to come to their own decision.

Ask the children to think of the words they could use to help their pal to think of all the possible solutions. Ask volunteers to raise a hand and tell you what they think. Make a list of all their suggestions – whether you think they will work or not. Read through the final list and talk about which are good ideas and which would work well.

> You could say:
>
> What could you do?
> What would happen then?
> Can you think of another way?
> Suppose that didn't work, what then?
> Have you thought how he would feel?
> Would that make your pal angry?
> Could you really do that?
> Who could help you?

Read through the words underneath that a buddy might say. (You could write them out on the board or flipchart.) Ask the children to work in pairs and decide which are good and which are not?

> 'What was your other idea?'
> 'I think your best plan is to...'
> 'No, don't do that, it won't work...'
> 'So let's think of what you said, you could... or this...
> 'Which do you think is best?'
> 'Leave it to me, I'll sort it out.'
> 'Let's go over what you said again.'
> 'Whatever you do, don't do that.'

Remind the children that they are there to support and befriend their pal, NOT to make their decisions for them.

Helping your pal to make decisions

Read the previous page to set the scene.

Duplicate the list and ask each pair to role-play the one of their choice. Explain that they have to show their role-play to the whole class.

Ask the children to work in pairs and allow ten minutes to practice. Give a minutes' warning before asking volunteers to show their role-play.

You are in the playground with your pal. She wants you to sort out her problem with a bully and has pointed out the boy that she says is doing this. You mustn't get involved. How can you get your pal to come to a good decision about this? What words will you say?

You pal brings a lunch box to school each day and eats in the dinner hall with the children having a school meal. She wants to have a school meal and asks you to help her to do this. What can you say to help her to come to the right decision about what to do?

You are in the classroom, peer teaching, when you see your pals number book with lots of mistakes. She tells you not to look at that book because she hates number work. She asks you to tell her teacher to stop making her do this work. What can you say?

You see your pal take a ball from the PE stand to play with in the playground. This isn't allowed. You ask to see it; she hides it and says it's hers. You don't want to hurt her feelings, but what can you say to help her to realise that she shouldn't do this. How can you help her to come to the right decision to put it back and not take it again?

Discuss these role-plays and question the decisions the children have identified.

Help them to identify good ideas and solutions. Praise them for their work.

Feelings of both buddy and pal

You know that it is very important to get on with your pal and for your pal to get on with you.

Tell the children that today you are all going to think about the kinds of things they can say to make sure that their relationship with their pal is a good, friendly one. Ask them to finish the sentence: 'I could say things like…'

> **I could say**
>
> Hi Smiler!
> How's my best pal today?
> Hey pal, how's things?
> You're looking good today.
> I'm so glad to see you.
> Come over here and talk to me.

Now ask them to think of things they might say that would make their pal feel down or fed-up, things such as 'Oh, it's you again,' 'What's up with you today?', or 'I can see you're fed-up.'

Explain that the things on their positive list will make both themselves and their pal feel friendly and happy, but saying negative things will make them both feel down. Help the children to understand that if they go towards their pal with a light heart and a positive attitude, this will influence the pal and make for a good session.

Ask the children to work in pairs to decide the best thing to say in each of these situations, A or B.

Your pal has been crying.	A What, you're crying again?
	B Come over here and I'll cheer you up.
Your pal hates his dinner.	A Are you upset again about dinner?
	B Why don't you just eat the things you like?
She's still on the same reader.	A What, still on this same book?
	B You've nearly finished this one, let's read some together.
She's forgotten her dinner money.	A Don't worry, you can bring it tomorrow.
	B Forgotten it again, you silly girl?

Ask them to make up one more scenario like this, to write it down and role-play it. Ask volunteers to show their role-play to the whole class.

Feelings of both buddy and pal

Use the activities on the previous page to set the scene.

Remind the children that they have a very important part to play as a role model to their pal. If their pal sees them happy and glad to be at school, with a friendly smile, some of this will influence the pal.

When you do that, it makes me feel really happy.

Explain the technique of 'It makes me feel' which can be useful when with a pal who is either over excited or displaying other feelings. This technique is about using the behaviour, not the child, as the target for the remark, for example, if a child is looking down, a good thing to say is, 'When you look sad like that it makes me feel…' rather than emphasising that the pal is looking miserable.

Look at these examples. Choose the best – A or B.

Your pal is kicking the tree bark because she is angry.	A When you do that it makes me feel upset too. B Don't do that, it'll spoil the tree.
Your pal has remembered all her spelling words.	A All of them – this makes me feel really great. B Have you, oh good.
Your pal is looking cross and fed-up because she didn't know her spellings.	A Come on, try harder next week. B It makes me feel sad to see you upset, I know you tried to learn them, they were hard.
Your pal has forgotten her PE kit again.	A I guess you feel fed-up about that, when I forget mine I get cross with myself too. B Tell the teacher, she won't be very cross.
Your pal is going to be Mary in the Christmas play.	A It makes me feel pleased too – isn't that great! B Oh yeah, I was in the play once.

Ask the children to work in their groups and make up scenarios similar to these, but writing in only positive and encouraging remarks which emphasise how they themselves feel. Ask each group to display their written scenario on a table and ask everyone to go around the room and read them all.

As a whole class, use these scenarios for comment and discussion.

Role models

Explain to the children that they are role models to their pals. Do they understand exactly what a role model is? Ask volunteers to say what they think.

> A role-model is a person who is looked up to by others as a good example of that role.

Can you come to an agreed definition?

Ask the children to work in pairs and to make a list of all the things they can do, be or say to show they are good examples of a pupil of your school.

Come together and talk about their lists. Have they mentioned school uniform, clean and neat, tidy hair, a smile, consideration for others, a pleasant manner?

Make one inclusive list of all the attributes of a good role model for your school. Display this list on your buddy board under the heading 'Role model for… School'.

Ask each child to draw themselves in their school uniform and write under their picture the things that they say, do and have, which demonstrate that they are a good role model for the school.

Ask the children to put a copy of their role model list in their folder.

Role model for Ashton Primary School

I am in school uniform and have my PE bag and my lunch box. I am smiling because I am happy. I try to do the right things and not to get into trouble. I work hard with my lessons and am polite to the teachers.

Role models

Tell the children that it is very important for buddies to be a good role model for their peers. Ask them to think of what this means and to give examples of what a good role model at your school would look like.

Explain to them that it is not so much about how they look, about dressing well in uniform, but more about their personal qualities, the way they act, move and speak. Ask them to think about what personal qualities a good role model would display. Ask them to work in pairs and to make a list. In Circle Time, ask each pair to read out their list while a scribe writes this down on the board. When a second pair says the same word, put 'plus 1' alongside it. At the end you should have a list of words, many of which will have a tally number at the side. Ask someone to re-write this list – perhaps on the computer, with the qualities in numerical order and display it on the buddy board.

> **Good role model qualities.**
>
> The numbers show how many of us chose these.
>
> | | |
> |---|---|
> | consideration | 6 |
> | thinking of others | 2 |
> | empathy | 4 |
> | sympathy | 7 |
> | understanding | 10 |
> | patience | 6 |
> | tolerance | 2 |
> | staying power | 1 |
> | thoughtfulness | 6 |
> | kindness | 20 |
> | helpfulness | 23 |

Ask each child to choose three of the above personal qualities and write a sentence or two about how they could display this quality to their pal. For example, if they chose 'patience' they might write:

> When my pal is doing her reading, I wait until she has tried to say the word before I step in and try to help her. This way she knows she has time to think about the word and doesn't get flustered. If she really doesn't know it, I help her out by sounding out the letters.

Ask volunteers to read out their sentences in the next Circle Time.

Remind them that these personal qualities of a role model extend to other roles, that of a son or daughter, pupil, neighbour, friend and member of the wider community.

Review and reflect

Spend a little time reflecting on the work the children have done. Ask them to think about what they didn't know before they started this section of activities.

Look at the buddy board and read the new work.

Ask the children what they think they have learned from these activities.

Help them to understand that the activities will also help them to be a better person in other roles of their life and that the skills they are learning are the skills of being a good citizen.

Ask each child to draw a picture of themselves doing something outside school to show they are being good citizens. Ask them to write a caption or speech bubble to say what they are doing in their picture.

In my picture I am picking up some rubbish from the front of my garden. People let it drop when they walk by and it looks a mess. I always take my litter home and put it in the dustbin.

Anton

Section 6: A Successful Buddy

In this section the activities are designed to help the buddy think through his responsibilities, recognise exactly what he is contracting to do for his pal and how he can keep records to evaluate this

> Manifesto
>
> Badges
>
> Contract
>
> First meeting
>
> Reporting back – a self-evaluation exercise
>
> Buddy handbook

Manifesto

In Circle Time, tell the children that they are almost at the end of their training to be a good school buddy. There is just one section to go and that is all about themselves and what they have to offer.

Explain that politicians have to offer a manifesto when they want to be a member of parliament and that the manifesto is a written document that tells everyone what they will do if they become an MP. It usually has a photo of the person and says quite a lot about the kind of person they are – their personal qualities.

Explain that today's task is for them to write their manifesto to be a buddy. Ask the children to think about which of their good qualities they would like to include in their manifesto.

> ## A Manifesto
>
> about me, what I am like
> friendly and warm
> easy to talk to
> confident
> positive and encouraging
> understanding and sensible
> helpful and respectful
> reliable and supportive
> what I can do
> how I could help a buddy
> what I am good at
> my good qualities
> my promise.

Ask volunteers to tell you and jot down a list of what they say. Display this list so that the children can easily see it. Read through the list with the children and ask them if they think they can add anything more.

Ask the children to get a piece of paper and to write the heading 'My Manifesto' and to draw a picture of themselves on it.

Underneath the picture ask them to write all about themselves, using the ideas from the class list. Remind them to look through their buddy folder for ideas of what to write.

Ask them to finish with the sentence: 'I think I would be a good buddy because…'

Manifesto

Use the activities in the first three paragraphs on the facing page as a starter for this session. Read through the qualities that the children have suggested.

Ask volunteers to (or you yourself) write these down on playing card sized cards and spread them out where everyone can see. Ask the children to suggest any additions and then try to put the cards in order of importance. Allow discussion and disagreement.

Ask each child to make his own list, using the cards, omitting any that he thinks are not appropriate or relevant. Now ask the children to look at their lists and to draw a ring around the two most important qualities that they already have. Ask them to draw a line underneath any that they need to work at. Ask them to think back to Section 2 where they thought about the aims of the buddy scheme and the skills they would need to be successful buddies.

> ## My personal qualities
>
> warm and caring
> thoughtful
> good memory
> interested in others
> positive attitude.
>
> ## My skills
>
> good at communication
> good listener
> can show I am interested
>
> ## My feelings
>
> happiness, joy
> fun
> caring for others
> empathy.

Ask them to look in their buddy folder and to bring out anything about aims and skills. Ask them to incorporate these aims and skills into their manifesto list. Ask them to think about the feelings work they did in Section 3. Ask them to incorporate some of these into their manifesto list.

Ask each child to write their own manifesto, incorporating some of these new ideas into it. Ask them to finish by writing a sentence of intent; what they will endeavour to do as a good school buddy. Remind them that this manifesto tells other people a lot about them. It must be true. Could they show it to their friends and family who may be able to suggest other items to include? Display all the manifestos on tables around the room and ask the children to vote for one to display on the buddy board. Tell the children to put theirs in their folder.

Badges

Tell the children that you think it a good idea if they have some identification to show when they are on duty. If they wear some kind of badge, other people will know that they have the right to be in certain areas of the school. It will also help their pal and the pal's teacher to know that they are responsible for their pal when wearing their badge.

When they are not being a buddy, they can keep their badge in their buddy folder.

Talk about:

> ▶ the size of the badge
>
> ▶ the design
>
> ▶ the shape
>
> ▶ the colours.

Ask the children if they can think of any particular logo that would look good on a Buddy Badge.

Ask them to draw their preferred design on a piece of paper; the kind of badge they would be proud to wear.

You may like to choose one design to submit to a company who could make sufficient for every child in the class or help the children to make their own badge using card with a sealed cover of plastic or sellotape.

Contract

Tell the children that you want them to make a contract – a promise of how they will carry out their duties of being a good buddy.

Ask them to tell you some of the things they have learned during this training programme and suggest they include these, and more, in their contract.

> **Contract**
>
> when we will meet
> where we meet
> our main responsibilities
> our friendliness
> our confidentiality.

Each contract, on good quality paper or card, can be illustrated or decorated as the children wish, using crayon, paint, felt tips or other media.

Display these contracts in the classroom or take down all the work from the buddy board and display them there for everyone in the school to see.

First meeting

Explain to the children that this first meeting will be the most important and will set the tone for future meetings. Talk through your arrangements for the first meeting, where and when it will be held and who will be there.

Ask the children to think of the meeting in four stages:

Stage 1 is where they first see their pal and where they introduce themselves.

Stage 2 is where they talk to their pal and find out a little about them.

Stage 3 is where they say how they can help their pal.

Stage 4 is saying goodbye for now and reminding their pal of the next meeting.

> ## First stage
>
> I would say...
> My name is Jack and I am going to be your buddy. I am in Year ... and I really enjoy being at this school. I like to play football and my favourite lesson is English. I think we are going to get on really well.

Ask the children to imagine this meeting. Can they think what they will say first?

Ask them all to get paper and pencil and write down what they will say to their pal in stage 1 of this meeting.

Collect up the papers and ask volunteers to comment on what each child has written. Keep the papers that give a good starter to this meeting and discard the rest.

Do the same with the other three stages, collecting up the useful ideas from the children.

Ask the children to help you to make a list of the best things to say in each stage and ask someone to write this out or computerise it to go on the buddy board.

First meeting

Go through the activities on the facing page as a starter for this session.

Remind the children about all the skills they now have that they can use to help their pal to feel good about being in your school.

Explain that there are good opening sentences that will help their pal to get a conversation started. Remind them about the questioning techniques and ask volunteers to tell you any good ways of 'interviewing' their pal. Explain that a conversation is a bit like playing tennis, you take turns speaking and listening and following up what the other one says.

Remind your children that there are barriers to good buddying – things that will stop them from having a good conversation, for example: noise, too many people around, something exciting happening, no interest and no eye contact. Ask the children to work in pairs. Give out small pieces of paper of playing card size and ask the children to write down any barriers they can think of, each on a separate piece.

> ## You could say...
>
> Tell me about...
> Can you describe...
> How do you feel when...
> I've got one brother, have you?
> My sister is Jodie, have you got any sisters?
> Do you know about playgrounds?
> I like football, what do you like?
> I support Southampton, which team do you support?
> I like to go swimming, do you? Where do you swim?
> Do you watch TV? I like...
> What do you like to eat best?
> We go skating sometimes, have you ever been?
> I like your shoes, where did you get them?
> I like to listen to music, do you? What kind of music do you like?

Come back together as a class and collect the papers. Read each one and either lay it out on the floor in the centre of the circle, put it on a table or pin it on a board, making a line of papers with different ideas. Put repeated ideas on the top of the original. With the repeats, ask the children to help you to choose the best, or write out one which encapsulates the idea. Ask the children to suggest how these can be displayed in order of importance – the worst barrier to a good conversation first.

Reporting back – a self-evaluation exercise

After the first meeting of the buddy with his pal it would be useful to do this self-evaluation exercise. An amended version of this page is duplicated in the Appendix so that you can easily photocopy it for later self-evaluation.

With younger buddies you could go through the questions in Circle Time and ask volunteers to tell you their responses.

With older buddies you could duplicate it on two sides of A4, ask each buddy to complete it anonymously and use their responses as a discussion document.

How did the meeting go?

What did you like about your pal?

What have you already learned about your pal?

Do you think you will get on well and form a partnership?

Do you think your pal has any worries?

If yes, list them here.

In which ways do you think you can help your pal?

Were you able to make the meeting fun? If so, how?

Did you find any aspect of the meeting difficult? If yes, explain this.

What skills do you think you need to improve so that you can be a better buddy?

Do you think you will enjoy being a buddy?

What will you enjoy most?

Buddy handbook

Tell the children that they will need an up-to-date handbook to help them to do their buddying. Remind them of all the work they have done in this training programme, some of which will be in their buddy folders, some on the buddy board.

Ask them to think about what they will need in their buddy handbooks. Can they think of some headings that will help them to get started? Ask volunteers to suggest these and make a note of all of them, whether you think they are appropriate or not.

Read through the list, discussing the usefulness of the items and discarding those that are not really appropriate.

Explain that the first part of the book will include details of their pal and reminders of their roles and responsibilities.

> ## Buddy handbook
>
> my pal's name
> their details
> their class & teacher
> times/dates of meetings
> note about organisation
> aims of the buddy scheme
> my responsibilities
> note of relationship boundaries
> list of skills I need
> questioning techniques
> list of things to talk about
> note about confidentiality
> what to do with serious problems
> names of who to report to
> blank pages for records.

The second part of the book is where they will keep a short but clear note of each meeting, a kind of diary; to remind them of what went on, how the meeting went, things to remember to do and things to check up on next time. This is confidential, so remind buddies not to write down anything that could breach confidentiality should someone else find their handbook and read it. Suggest they use a code or abbreviations for this kind of entry.

The third part of the buddy handbook is where they will keep their self-evaluation sheets. This self-evaluation is private to them and is to help them to recognise where they can improve their buddying skills. There is a photocopiable sheet on page 100.

Explain that their buddy folders are to be discontinued and ask them to look through all the papers they have in them. Can they use some of this information to put into their buddy handbook? Use your buddy board for other ideas.

Loose leaf folders would be ideal for buddy handbooks.

Ask the children to section out their books, number the pages and to get started by transferring information from their buddy folder into the handbooks. They can either re-write this or cut and paste.

Children may need practise in writing their diary pages about each meeting with their pal. Talk them through this scenario and ask them to pretend it was their meeting with their pal and to write it out as a diary entry in note form, recording the meeting.

> They met in the pal's classroom just before play and he could see that his pal was very upset. She said that last playtime she had been playing with some children from her class and someone from another class came and punched her and knocked her over. She asked the buddy to go and sort out the problem for her.

> ## September 20th
>
> Met pal in classroom, she looked upset.
> Tried to cheer her up; she said someone pushed her over last playtime.
> Wanted me to go sort out problem. Explained couldn't do this, but talked about what happened. Asked her to think about what she could have done. She could have told playground teacher, but end of playtime. She said could have told her own teacher. She cheered up then – not really hurt.
> Asked about her work - she smiled - said she had a star for good writing.
> Said, 'So long'. Meet next week. * Must remember to ask about this next time.

Ask the children to record the event in three paragraphs, the start of their meeting, what happened during the meeting and how the meeting ended. Ask them to remember to include details of the feelings of the pal and any follow-up.

Section 7: From the Pal's Perspective

In this section the activities are designed to help the pal to understand the boundaries of her buddy's role and how their meetings will be organised. There is a suggested format for evaluation to enable each pal to assess the effectiveness of her buddy.

First meeting on pal's pre-school visit

After pals have started school

Pal's evaluation of buddy

First meeting on pal's pre-school visit

The two teachers concerned will arrange the pairing of buddy to pal.
Before the pals start school, tell them about the buddy system. Explain that
their buddy is an older pupil at the school who will help them to settle into
school and help to show them around.

Tell them that you will arrange a time for them to meet their buddy and get to
know them. Explain that their buddy will:

- ▸ meet them once a week on Monday mornings (give exact details)
- ▸ be able to come and help them with their work occasionally (give details)
- ▸ talk over any problems they might have
- ▸ talk to them about the things buddies can help them with
- ▸ act as a kind of special classroom helper to be someone who can help.

Tell the children that they have a role to play in all of this. Their responsibilities
include:

- ▸ talking to their buddy
- ▸ listening to their buddy
- ▸ being friendly
- ▸ getting to know each other
- ▸ working together as a kind of partnership
- ▸ telling worries
- ▸ talking over solutions to problems
- ▸ co-operating when their buddy is peer teaching.

Tell the children that their buddy is a special kind of friend, but

- ▸ not a teacher
- ▸ not there to give them orders
- ▸ not in charge of them
- ▸ not someone they meet out of school.

After pals have started school

Arrange for the buddies and pals to meet as soon as possible after the pals start school.

If you have a staggered entry to infant/first school, try to make it possible for the buddy to take the pal out to the playground on their first day. If break times coincide this should not prove a problem for the timetable, otherwise special arrangements will have to be made. On this first occasion, when the children have arrived in the playground, the buddies could be bystanders while pals play together. Less secure pals may need their buddies to stay with them for this first play.

My buddy

My buddy is called Malik and he is in Year 6. He has brown hair and blue eyes and likes football.

Arrange the first real meeting as soon as all the new entrants have started school. You may like to allow the buddy to sit and talk with their pal in the classroom. This will enable the pal to talk about their new classroom and show the buddy around. It would be a good idea for the two to choose and share a book together, for the pal to draw a picture for the buddy to keep or vice versa.

Remind the pals that the buddies have their own classroom work to do and their own friends to play with and that if they share a playground they must not expect their buddies to spend all their time with their pals. They are only there for them when they are wearing their buddy badge.

After the first real meeting, ask young pals to draw a picture of themselves with their buddy, copy their buddy's name and copy or write a caption. Older pals can write about their buddy and about the meeting.

Pal's evaluation of buddy

Roundabout the first half term of the buddy scheme it is a good idea to get feedback from the pals about the effectiveness of the buddy scheme.

You can do this orally with the youngest children or provide an evaluation sheet for older children to complete. (See Appendix.) You may like to share this evaluation with the buddy.

In Circle Time explain that you want them to tell you about how they feel about having a buddy in school. Start by asking them to finish the sentence: 'I like my buddy because…'

> My buddy helped me when I felt upset because my friend wouldn't play with me.

Collect their responses to make a list.

Now ask them to tell you one thing they know about their buddy. In the circle ask children to finish the sentence: 'I know that my buddy…'

Talk with the children about any ways in which buddies have been able to help them. Can volunteers tell you one specific occasion when a buddy has helped their pal in your class? Collect examples and talk about them.

Ask them all to draw a picture of their buddy and write the ending to the sentence, 'I think it is good to have a buddy because…'

You might like to encourage this kind of evaluation again after the next half term.

My buddy is Nick

I think it's good to have a buddy because they can talk to you and help you to know things about school.

Appendix

Effective listening skills

Buddy self-evaluation sheet

Pal's self-evaluation sheet

Suggested letters

Suggested Certificates

Effective listening skills

These skills should form the basis of your class's list; it is in no particular order. Your children may well use different words and terms, but in essence the list should include the following:

- ▸ sit opposite to your pal

- ▸ look at your pal's face

- ▸ lean slightly towards them and keep good eye contact

- ▸ use good, positive body language

- ▸ give them your undivided attention – don't let anyone or anything interrupt

- ▸ for a very private conversation, make sure you are in a private place

- ▸ really listen to the words they are saying – concentrate

- ▸ make sure you understand what they are meaning to say

- ▸ show by your face how you are reacting to what they say

- ▸ show you are interested in their problem

- ▸ say 'Mmm' or 'Yes' and nod and smile to encourage them to continue

- ▸ show sympathy for their problem

- ▸ put yourself in their place to try to understand their feelings

- ▸ don't interrupt, wait until they finish before you say anything

- ▸ don't worry if there is a long silence

- ▸ if you don't understand, say something such as, 'I think you're trying to say... Am I right?'

- ▸ don't offer a solution, ask them what they think would be a good idea

- ▸ list their ideas and get them to think which is the best

- ▸ don't argue with them, help them to come to a sensible decision or conclusion.

How did the meeting go?

What do you like about your pal?

What do you know about your pal?

Have you formed a partnership? Yes/No
If no, what can you do to make this happen?

Do you think your pal has any worries? Yes/No
If yes, list them here.

In which ways do you think you can help your pal?

Do you find any aspect of the meetings difficult?   Yes/No
If yes, explain this.

What skills do you think you need to improve so that you
can be a better buddy?

Do you think you are helping your pal with your peer teaching?
Yes/No If yes, how? If no, how can you become better at this.

Do you enjoy being a buddy? Yes/No

What do you enjoy most?

My name is

I like my buddy because...

My buddy helped me when...

My buddy peer teaches me and...

I think _____ **is a good buddy because...**

I try to be a good pal to my buddy when I....

Dear Parents

Peer Buddy Scheme

We have decided to operate a buddy scheme in our school and this letter is to explain how it will work. We think that a buddy scheme will help the youngest children in school (called 'pals') to integrate and to feel they have someone they can talk to about school and how it works. Buddies will gain increased self-confidence, enhanced communication skills and a sense of responsibility.

Older children enjoy caring for younger ones; they get pleasure and increased self-esteem in being in such a supportive role. Younger children are very receptive to older friends and in some cases are more ready to accept the teaching and parenting that such a role provides.

The older children (the buddies) will complete a training programme during the summer term in their penultimate year, becoming buddies in their last year. This training will form part of their personal, social, health and citizenship education, enabling them to offer support and guidance to new children to the school.

Being a peer buddy will also enhance their status during their last year at our school, giving them valuable skills that they will find useful in their next stage of education.

As new children enter our school they will be allocated a buddy from Year… This buddy will meet with their pal each Monday morning and they will spend ten minutes together. There will also be a small element of peer teaching incorporated into the scheme.

We will be explaining the scheme more fully at the annual meeting.

Peer Buddy Scheme

A peer buddy scheme can be beneficial to the whole school. It is thought that peer relationships provide a greater understanding between children, especially where one is older and providing support and one is younger gaining support. It helps the new entrants in school to integrate and to feel they have someone they can talk to about school and how it works. Buddies will gain increased self-confidence, enhanced communication skills and a sense of responsibility.

Older children enjoy caring for younger ones; they get pleasure and increased self-esteem in being in such a supportive role. Younger children are very receptive to older friends and are normally more than ready to accept the teaching and parenting that such a role provides.

The buddies will complete a training programme during the summer term in their penultimate year, becoming buddies in their last year. This training will form part of their personal, social health and citizenship education, enabling them to offer support and guidance to new entrants. Being a peer buddy will also enhance their status during their last year at our school, giving them valuable skills that they will find useful in their next stage of education.

The training programme will be the responsibility of the teachers of Year… while the implementation of the programme will be the responsibility of Year… teachers, who will also act as co-ordinators should there be any worries or concerns of the new entrants that need teacher intervention.

As new children enter school they will be allocated a buddy from Year… This buddy will meet the new children each Monday morning and spend ten minutes with them. There will also be a small element of peer teaching incorporated in the scheme to allow buddies to help children with their reading and number skills.

A celebration at the end of the school year will enable buddies and pals to share their work and appreciation of each other's roles.

Suggested letter to parents of new entrants in the pre-entry information packs given out when children are registered for school

Appendix

Dear Parent

Buddy Scheme

We have a buddy scheme in operation at this school. This means that one of the Year… children will be chosen to help your child to settle into school, to 'show them the ropes', to talk to them about the way the school is organised and help them with any little problems. We call the older child a 'buddy' and your child a 'pal'.

When your child starts school in September a buddy from Year… will be on hand to help your child to settle into school. The buddies will first meet their pals on the pre-school visits and we will try to make an opportunity for you to meet them as you drop off or collect your child.

Buddies have been trained to do this befriending and will know how and when to help and advise your child.

Buddies will meet their pals in the playground every Monday morning for the first few weeks of term. Occasionally buddies will be able to visit their pals in their classroom to talk with them about their work and help them to practise new skills.

You will be able to talk more fully about how this buddy/pal scheme works at the pre-school meeting with your child's class teacher.

Suggested letter to parents/carers of newly trained buddies

Dear Parent

You will know that we have a buddy/pal scheme in our school so that the older children can help new entrants to settle into school and to find their way about.

This term your child has been trained to look out for, and deal with, the kinds of things that a buddy can do to help new and young children when they first start at our school. This training has helped your child to understand the responsibilities that they are undertaking and to realise the needs of new entrants to school.

Next term, when your child is in the oldest age group in school, they will put into practice the skills they have been learning. They will meet their pal during Monday morning play and be on hand to talk to them about school and ways in which they can help them to settle. They will answer any of their pal's questions and tell them about the customs of our school.

Occasionally your child will also be able to visit their pal's classroom to admire their work and help them to practise reading, number or other skills. This kind of peer teaching will benefit your child by giving her/him the opportunity to pass on their knowledge about school as well as raising her/his status as one of the most responsible pupils in school.

You will have an opportunity to talk to your child's teacher about this at our first open evening.

Certificate for participation in buddy training programme

Presented by .... school

Awarded to

....

for successfully participating in the buddying training programme

Date ....

Best Buddy Certificate

Presented by .... school

Presented to

....

Celebrating working with a pal in the
school buddy scheme

Date ....

Resources

Bornman, J., Collins, M. & Maines, B. *Just the Same on the Inside*, Lucky Duck Publishing Ltd.

Collins, M. (2001) *Circle Time for the Very Young*, Lucky Duck Publishing Ltd.

Collins, M. (2001) *Because We're Worth It,* Lucky Duck Publishing Ltd.

Collins, M. (2002) *Circling Round Citizenship,* Lucky Duck Publishing Ltd.

Collins, M. (2002) *Because I'm Special,* Lucky Duck Publishing Ltd.

Collins, M. (2003) *Enhancing Circle Time for the Very Young,* Lucky Duck Publishing Ltd.

Collins, M. (2004) *Circling Safely,* Lucky Duck Publishing Ltd.

Collins, M. (2004) *But is it Bullying?* Lucky Duck Publishing Ltd.

Cowie, H. & Sharp, S. (1996) *Peer Counselling in Schools – A Time to Listen*, David Fulton.

DfEE (2001) *Promoting Children's Mental Health within Early Years and School Settings.*

Smith, C. (2002) *B.E.S.T. Buddies*, Lucky Duck Publishing Ltd.

Topping, K (1996) Reaching Where Adults Cannot; Peer Education and Peer Counselling. *Educational Psychology in Practice.* 11,4,23-30.

Wetton, N. & Collins, M. (2003) *Pictures of Health*, Belair Publications Ltd.

Margaret Collins is a former headteacher in infant/first schools. She is now a Visiting Fellow in the School of Education at the University of Southampton. She researches children's perceptions of health education topics, writes and co-writes teaching materials for children, books and articles on personal, social, health and citizenship education (PSHCE).